Memories
of
Newbury

Part of the
Memories
series

*The Publishers would like to thank the following companies for supporting
the production of this book*

Main Sponsors

Camp Hopson & Company Limited

Newbury Building Society

Dreweatt Neate

Gardner Leader

Husseys Bakery

Newbury College

NRS Limited

First published in Great Britain by True North Books Limited
Units 3 - 5 Heathfield Industrial Park
Elland West Yorkshire
HX5 9AE
Tel. 01422 377977
© Copyright: True North Books Limited 1999

ISBN 1 900463 79 2

*Text, design and origination by True North Books Limited
Printed and bound by The Amadeus Press Limited*

Memories are made of this

Memories. We all have them: people, places and events, some good and some bad. Our memories of the place where we grew up are usually tucked away in a very special place in our mind. The best are probably connected with our childhood and youth, when we longed to be grown up and paid no attention to adults who told us to enjoy being young, as these were the best years of our lives. We look back now and realise that they were right.

Old photographs bring our memories flooding back - coronations and celebrations; talking pictures, Technicolour and television; the war years, rationing, and the shared hopes and fears which created such a warm community spirit; buying things made of nylon and plastic; fashions which took trouserbottoms and hemlines from drainpipes and mini-skirts to the other extreme; Doris Day, Acker Bilk, Elvis Presley and the Beatles; the jitterbug, the tango and discos; Ford Populars and Minis; decimalisation. Life changed so much over the years. Some changes were big, some small; some altered our lives in ways we never anticipated. Who in the early days of motoring could have foreseen the motorways and traffic systems of the latter decades of the 20th century? Did any of us realise, when we first saw a computer, what a tremendous impact they would have on our lives? Self-service supermarkets and frozen food made our lives easier - but at the expense of our friendly little corner shops. Nostalgia is always such a mixture of feelings . . . We hope that the collection of pictures in this book will remind you of happy days in bygone eras - and who knows, you might even have been there when one of the photographs was taken!

Contents

Newbury through the years

No town can avoid change. Newbury, once a small market town, has diversified from its traditional industries of clothing and farming to enter the third millennium as a thriving commercial centre. Although some people still regret the disappearance of the cattle market, the King's Arms, Wharf House and other features, there is no escaping the impact of lifestyle changes that affect the whole nation. There is a saying at Camp Hopson that 'If you are standing still then you are moving backwards', and arguably this applies to towns as well as to organisations. The pace of life in post-war Britain called for new roads to take increased traffic, modern office blocks to house hi-tech businesses, and the convenience of indoor shopping and multi-storey car parks. Some familiar landmarks had to make way for developments, others found a new role to play, and the town took on a slightly different character; while alongside these changes many old traditions have carried on, with such institutions as the market, the fair, the Agricultural Show and the Boxing Day Meet still as popular as ever with the younger generation.

But Newbury is not just about streets and buildings, it is also about people: the families and individuals - from the legendary Jack of Newbury onwards - who helped create the town. Some of Newbury's great characters have found their way into this book - the Camp and the Hopson families; the controversial Jimmy Tufnail who gave us our first cinema; Elsie Kimber, our first woman mayor; Jack Hole, the owner of the famous Tudor Restaurant who contributed to the life of the town in so many ways; our allies from across the Atlantic who were part of our lives for so many years; our own gallant Farmers' Boys, the Royal Berkshire Regiment; and many more besides. In these pages you will find pictures of Newbury before, during and after the Great War - pictures which we hope will stir memories for all those readers who lived in Newbury during these years, and at the same time provide, for those too young to remember, an insight into the town as their parents and grandparents knew it. Newbury is and always has been a town of great character; and whatever changes the next generations may choose to effect, we trust that its character will never be lost.

Around the town centre

> *By 1960 ten and a half million families had a television*

Shop canopies were clearly the in-thing in the mid 1950s; a stranger to Newbury armed with an aerial photograph of the main streets would have been able to plan out a shopping expedition in advance with the greatest of ease! Readers with the eyesight of a hawk may be able to decipher the name of the film showing at the Regal at the time of this picture; in fact it was Come Back Little Sheba, a rather unmemorable American film starring Burt Lancaster, about an ex-alcoholic who on top of everything else had rotten luck with women. 'That girl in their house spelled trouble!' was the publicity tag - hardly one to draw in huge audiences, perhaps, at a time when cinemas were already struggling to tempt viewers away from the small screen in the corner of the living room; by 1960, ten and a half million families in Britain would have a TV. The Regal was opened in 1927; it subsequently became part of the Associated British Cinemas chain, but closed in 1962 and was later demolished.

In view of the sweeping changes that have affected other parts of Cheap Street, this particular view, hinging as it does on the Municipal Buildings at one end and the Post Office the other, is remarkably similar today. The alterations that have come about in between these two enduring landmarks are relatively unobtrusive. Certain of the buildings on the left-hand side of Cheap Street have been replaced, and further down in Market Place we now have an entrance to the Kennet Centre; but the unusual juxtaposition of rooflines nearest the camera on the left-hand edge of the picture, where

the triple gabled house adjoins the low, battlemented frontage of the Catherine Wheel Inn, is still intact. At the time of writing the sign for Beynon Limited, facing us on Market Place, is still there, although the business itself is not - a sad loss for those country folk who used to rely on this shop for their traditional warm winter clothing.

Events of the 1930s

HOT OFF THE PRESS
The years of the 1930s saw Adolf Hitler's sickening anti-Jewish campaign echoed in the streets of Britain. On 19th October 1936 Oswald Mosley's 7,000-strong British Union of Fascists clashed head on with thousands of Jews and Communists in London, resulting in 80 people being injured in the ensuing battle. Mosley and his 'blackshirts' later rampaged through the streets beating up Jews and smashing the windows of their businesses.

GETTING AROUND
At the beginning of the decade many believed that the airship was the transport of the future. The R101 airship, however, loaded with thousands of cubic metres of hydrogen, crashed in France on its maiden flight in 1930. Forty-eight passengers and crew lost their lives. In 1937 the Hindenburg burst into flames - the entire disaster caught on camera and described by a distraught reporter. The days of the airship were numbered.

SPORTING CHANCE
In 1939 British racing driver Sir Malcolm Campbell hit the headlines when he captured the world's water-speed record for the third time in 'Bluebird' - all his cars were given the same name. A racing driver who set world speed records both on land and on water, Sir Malcolm established world land-speed records no fewer than nine times. His son Donald went on to set further records, tragically dying in 1967 when his speedboat - also named 'Bluebird' - crashed.

Above: This is the view that would have greeted an observer looking down Bartholomew Street from Blackboys Bridge during the 1950s; clearly celebrations of some kind were in the air when this photograph was taken, but as the exact date was not recorded we cannot be sure what the bunting and flags signified - the Festival of Britain, maybe? or the Coronation? The outlook today is not altogether dissimilar. You can still buy your bread at number 84 on the right, although it is no longer Edgington's, and further down the Nag's Head is still there, although the hop leaf sign, visible here, is not. The hop leaf was trademark of Simonds brewery, established in Reading in 1882 by the dynamic young William Blackall Simonds. It grew rapidly to become one of Berkshire's leading breweries, and its popularity then spread to the neighbouring counties. During the first half of the 20th century Simonds continued expanding and did its best to prevent the London breweries from establishing themselves in this part of the country, and by the second world war it was one of the area's leading brewers. By the time Simonds merged with the Courage group in 1960 it had a holding of over 1,200 licensed houses.

Right: If we look across the rooftops - where now no rooftops are, but the Kennet development instead - we can see Bartholomew Street; the Regal Cinema, set back slightly from the baseline of the adjoining properties and now the site of Pearl Assurance House (near Iceland) helps us situate ourselves. The houses in the foreground of the picture were demolished around Spring 1970 to make way for the shopping centre. Many people feel that a very great change in the character of the town centre has come about as a result of the high concentration of retail and commercial activity in the area, to the exclusion of family dwellings. In the early part of the century the centre of Newbury consisted of cottages mixed in with craftsmen's workshops, small businesses and shops, with the proprietors living above. Life went on there day and night, and strong bonds naturally developed between neighbours who lived and worked side by side. This sense of solidarity is no longer as strong, now that economic and social trends have to a large extent separated off our place of work from our homelife.

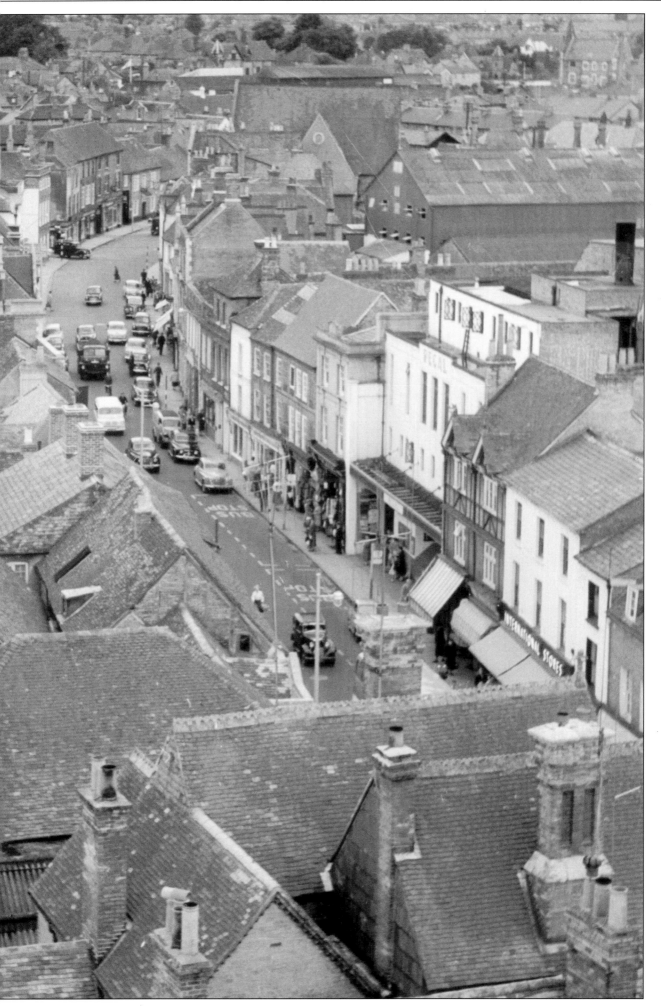

Next time you walk down Bartholomew Street, you might consider pausing for a moment to admire the three very realistic owls perched on high along the east side, and pondering just how much change has taken place beneath their wise and piercing gaze - and how much might be yet to come. Major demolition of parts of Bartholomew Street, along with parts of Market Street and buildings along the west side of Cheap Street, began in the Spring of 1970. Were the owls watching when Nias Garage disappeared in a cloud of dust and rubble, along with its neighbours? and did they see the Kennet development rise up in its

place, brick upon brick? Closer to their perch, the former Regal cinema bit the dust in 1968, to be replaced by Pearl Assurance House, untenanted at the time of writing and looking a trifle woebegone; other nationwide retail chains established themselves in new units along the street, and Bartholomew Street began to take on a more modern aspect.

Events of the 1930s

SCIENCE AND DISCOVERY
By observing the heavens, astronomers had long believed that there in the constellation of Gemini lay a new planet, so far undiscovered. They began to search for the elusive planet, and a special astronomical camera was built for the purpose. The planet Pluto was discovered by amateur astronomer Clyde Tombaugh in 1930, less than a year later.

WHAT'S ON?
In this heyday of the cinema, horrified audiences were left gasping at the sight of Fay Wray in the clutches of the giant ape in the film 'King Kong', released in 1933. Very different but just as gripping was the gutsy 1939 American Civil War romance 'Gone with the Wind'. Gable's parting words, 'Frankly, my dear, I don't give a damn' went down in history.

ROYAL WATCH
The talking point of the early 1930s was the affair of the Prince of Wales, who later became King Edward VIII, and American divorcee Wallis Simpson. Faced with a choice, Edward gave up his throne for 'the woman I love' and spent the remainder of his life in exile. Many supported him, though they might not have been as keen to do so if they had been aware of his Nazi sympathies, kept strictly under wraps at the time.

Above: Although the shop fronts have changed, the attractive gabled upper storeys of the buildings seen here have by and large remained unaltered. The more distant of the two Simonds' hop leaf signs on the right-hand side of Bartholomew Street marks the spot where the Eight Bells public house stood, now the Eight Bells coffee shop, with its picturesque 16th century frontage restored and immaculate. Across the road, the rather more solidly-styled Phoenix House also warrants a mention for the diverse roles it has played in Newbury's past: before being occupied by Newbury Rural District Council, this house was originally part of the Phoenix brewery which operated between 1842 and 1922, and it then served as Newbury's ARP control centre during the war. Vincents ironmongers, closer to the camera on the same side, was later taken over by Toomers of Northbrook Street, whose owner was responsible for opening the Regal cinema a little further along Bartholomew Street in 1927, in the building that had previously been the Red Stores. And a little nearer the camera on the opposite side is Woodlands Laundry, a go-ahead concern of its day which was apparently operating a fleet of delivery vehicles as early as the 1930s.

Below: Here we see London Road under water, with an intriguing sign behind the cluster of pedestrians advertising accommodation for 'motorist and cyclist' - which rather suggests that some of the many inns which used to stand along London Road did discriminate! Newbury has had its share of bad weather over the course of the 20th century. Few readers will remember the disastrous flooding on 7th January 1915, but those with long enough memories might recall the gales and torrential rain which wreaked havoc in September 1935, and the 12 inches snow which covered Newbury three winters later. The next decade brought more havoc: in 1947 sheep, cattle and crops were lost in the floods, and a meals-on-wheels operation organised by Jack Hole brought help to those worst affected. Then there was the Berkshire tornado in May 1950, and more heavy snow in 1952 . . . The exact date of this picture is unrecorded, but is known to be earlier than 1958. Freak weather generally makes for a dismal, if evocative, photograph; by contrast, some readers may remember that January 1940 brought an ice storm to the south of England which glazed tree branches and created some delightful scenes - though those there at the time will also remember how bitterly cold it was!

Below: This spot on Broadway is clearly destined to bear a landmark, although the form which that landmark takes has varied considerably over the years. At one time a wayside chapel stood here. The chapel later fell into disuse and was converted into houses during the 16th century. In due course the houses were demolished, and some years later, in 1828, Speenhamland Lamp was erected. This lamp continued to illuminate the junction, though not very brightly, until the town decided that it wanted to put a new clock and lamp here, to commemorate Queen Victoria's silver jubilee in 1887. In due course this was done, and the Jubilee Clock occupied the site between 1889 and 1929. The present clock tower then took over the position, and the Jubilee Clock was placed to one side. When war broke out it was sacrificed for the cause and is rumoured to have ended its days in Plenty's Eagle Ironworks along with the Russian gun which once stood in Victoria Park, where it yielded up an impressive five tons of good quality cast iron.

Bottom: All these buildings have gone, and even the old railway bridge has been replaced by a new re-aligned bridge to serve the relief road. The Railway Hotel survived until the 90s, but the Axe & Compass and W F Perry's furniture shop were demolished in the 1960s to make way for the new road. When Perry's first occupied these premises the roof still bore the legend The Newbury Cinema, a reminder that it was on that site that James Tufnail established Newbury's very first cinema. Opened in 1910 by the Mayor, Alfred Camp, it had 250 seats and charged 3d or 6d for adults and 1d or 2d for children. Within the space of a month, Newbury went from having no cinemas to having two; Newbury Picture Palace opened at 59 Northbrook Street, next to the Methodist Chapel, just 26 days later. The Picture Palace survived the relatively short-lived Newbury Cinema by many years, finally closing in 1931 because it could not be adapted for talkies. Its premises, too, have far outlasted those of its early rival; they are still there today, although with the building divided into two and occupied jointly, at the time of writing, by a men's outfitters and an estate agent, it bears little resemblance to a cinema.

Events of the 1930s

MELODY MAKERS
Throughout the 1930s a young American trombonist called Glenn Miller was making his mark in the world of music. By 1939 the Glenn Miller sound was a clear leader in the field; his clean-cut, meticulously executed arrangements of numbers such as 'A String of Pearls' and 'Moonlight Serenade' brought him fame across the world as a big-band leader. During a flight to England from Paris in 1944 Miller's plane disappeared; no wreckage was ever found.

THE WORLD AT LARGE
In India, Gandhi's peaceful protests against British rule were gathering momentum. The Salt Laws were a great bone of contention: forced to buy salt from the British government, thousands of protestors marched to the salt works, intending to take it over in the name of the Indian people. Policemen and guards attacked the marchers, but not one of them fought back. Gandhi, who earned for himself the name 'Mahatma' - Great Soul - was assassinated in 1948.

INVENTION AND TECHNOLOGY
With no driving tests or speed restrictions, 120,000 people were killed on the roads in Britain between the two world wars. In 1934 Percy Shaw invented a safety device destined to become familiar the world over: reflecting roadstuds. In dark or foggy conditions the studs that reflected light from the car's headlights kept traffic on the 'straight and narrow' and must over the years have saved many lives.

On the left of this picture is one of the great institutions of Newbury life throughout the mid-20th century; for more than 40 years the Tudor Restaurant provided a mouth-watering afternoon tea with cakes and pastries baked in its own bakery, while in the evening the fine timbered restaurant was a favourite banqueting venue or a regular meeting place for all manner of local clubs and societies, from the Rotary Club and the Round Table to the Camera Club and the Beekeepers and Arts Society. The Tudor Cafe

was also responsible for the catering at civic and private functions held at other locations in and around the town. In addition to feeding the people of Newbury, its owner Jack Hole contributed to the life of the town in an extraordinary number of ways. A talented photographer and founder of Newbury Camera Club, he became President of the Chamber of Trade (subsequently renamed the Chamber of Commerce), was a founder member of Fair Close Day Centre, and was elected Mayor in 1950. In recognition of his services to Newbury he was made a Freeman of the Borough in 1969. But on a daily basis it was his perhaps his cakes which the town appreciated most of all, and his departure from the Tudor Restaurant was a sad day indeed. The restaurant continued briefly under new ownership, then closed down. Today it is a shoe shop.

Above: Although there seems to be little moving traffic on this photograph, parked vehicles abound, making life tricky for the pedestrian. In 1955, before Northbrook Street was pedestrianised, it was not advisable to jaywalk across the street with your mind on what you wanted to buy at Camp Hopson - or you might never get there. In response to an alarming increase in the number of people killed and injured on Britain's roads in the years after the first world war, Mr Leslie Hore-Belisha came up with a scheme to make life safer for the pedestrian, and Newbury can claim the rather unusual distinction of being the first town in Britain, as opposed to city, to equip itself with Belisha beacons. Pedestrian crossings marked out by studs and yellow beacons were introduced nationally in 1934, and in Newbury in 1935. Like any new idea, we had to get used to them; at first beacons were placed in the middle of the road to make them easy for motorists to spot, and pedestrians had to be educated into using them. The first beacons were made of glass and made a wonderful target for little boys with stones, so the glass beacons were replaced by painted aluminium globes. Crossings got their stripes in 1951, and the beacons became plastic and began to wink in 1952.

> *Newbury was the first town to have Belisha Beacons installed*

Right: A number of familiar names have been captured on this snapshot of Cheap Street in 1957: Carters Dyers, which became Bolloms around the end of the decade; the old-established business of H Dolton & Son, corn merchants, which has been in existence for over 200 years, occupying buildings along the Wharf in the early 20th century, then vacating them, then acquiring Town Mills from Hovis in 1957 and finally moving out to Hermitage in 1972; and the Welcome cafe, which at the time of writing is an amusements arcade. Dolton's building has become a Chinese restaurant. Carters and its neighbours on both sides have become a whole parade of estate agents. However, although the businesses have changed and the canopies have disappeared, the properties themselves have survived - though a wider angled lens, taking in the other side of the street, would have told a very different story . . .

Two clear signs of things to come in this snapshot from 1959 are the L-plated Austin making its way down Northbrook Street, and the Leisure Kitchens delivery van parked outside Boots. Living standards were rising fast and home improvements were becoming a way of life for post-war home-makers. Many couples saved up assiduously for comforts and luxuries their parents had probably never dreamed of possessing - fitted kitchens, fitted carpets, central heating, modern bathroom suites, even a family car. Between 1953 and 1963 the number of cars in the country rose from one car for every twenty-four people to one

for every seven, and it continued to rise. Driving schools flourished during the 60s, with passing your test becoming a rite of passage for the younger generation. In fact the driving test, along with L-plates and provisional licences, was first introduced in 1935, initially on a voluntary basis; it then became compulsory, and everybody who had taken out their first driving licence since 1st April 1934 was obliged to take a test. The test fee was initially set at 7/6 (37.5p), but the Driving Test Organisation was so honest that when it discovered it had unintentionally made a profit of £16,000, it reduced the fee.

The clock shows half past four, so rush hour has barely begun; but even so traffic is nose to tail along Northbrook Street. With traffic as heavy as this, one can see that shopping in 1960 was becoming less of a pleasure and more of a chore, with the noise, the fumes and the difficulty in crossing the road between parked cars all too often combining to make a trip into town a tiring and stressful experience. How times have changed since the beginning of the century! Cars were still a novelty then; in fact, it is recorded that when 50 cars travelled through Newbury on 23rd April 1900 on the first lap of the Automobile Club's 1,000 mile trial,

crowds turned out just to see them. The novelty soon wore off, however; by 1904 there were 8,465 cars in Britain, and by 1938, with the number approaching two million, traffic had become enough of a problem in Newbury to justify introducing one-way systems, while the town's first traffic lights had been installed some five years previously at the junction by St Nicolas' Church.

Events of the 1940s

WHAT'S ON?
In wartime Britain few families were without a wireless set. It was the most popular form of entertainment, and programmes such as ITMA, Music While You Work and Workers' Playtime provided the people with an escape from the harsh realities of bombing raids and ration books. In 1946 the BBC introduced the Light Programme, the Home Service and the Third Programme, which gave audiences a wider choice of listening.

GETTING AROUND
October 1948 saw the production of Britain's first new car designs since before the war. The Morris Minor was destined for fame as one of the most popular family cars, while the four-wheel-drive Land Rover answered the need for a British-made off-road vehicle. The country was deeply in the red, however, because of overseas debts incurred during the war. The post-war export drive that followed meant that British drivers had a long wait for their own new car.

SPORTING CHANCE
American World Heavyweight Boxing Champion Joe Louis, who first took the title back in 1937, ruled the world of boxing during the 1930s and 40s, making a name for himself as unbeatable. Time after time he successfully defended his title against all comers, finally retiring in 1948 after fighting an amazing 25 title bouts throughout his boxing career. Louis died in 1981 at the age of 67.

Wartime

I n 1939 Britain's Prime Minister Neville Chamberlain had made his announcement to the waiting people of Britain that '...this country is at war with Germany.' The country rolled up its sleeves and prepared for the inevitable. This war would be different from other wars. This time planes had the ability to fly further and carry a heavier load, and air raids were fully expected. Air raid shelters were obviously going to be needed, and shelters were built on open places across the town.

By the time war was declared an army of volunteers of both sexes had already been recruited to form an Air Raid Protection service. At first ARP personnel were unpaid volunteers but when war broke out in September 1939 they became paid staff. It was their job to patrol specified areas, making sure that no chinks of light broke the blackout restrictions, checking the safety of local residents, being alert for gas attacks, air raids and unexploded bombs. The exceptional work done by Air Raid Wardens in dealing with incendiaries, giving first aid to the injured, helping to rescue victims from their bombed-out properties, clearing away rubble, and a thousand and one other tasks became legendary; during the second world war nearly as many private citizens were killed as troops - and many of them were the gallant ARP wardens.

At the beginning of the war Sir Anthony Eden, Secretary of State for War, appealed in a radio broadcast for men between 17 and 65 to make up a new force, the Local Defence Volunteers, to guard vulnerable points from possible Nazi attack. Within a very short time the first men were putting their names down. At first the new force had to improvise; there were no weapons to spare and men had to rely on sticks, shotguns handed in by local people, and on sheer determination . Weapons and uniforms did not become available for several months.

In July the Local Defence Volunteers was renamed the Home Guard, and by the following year were a force to be reckoned with. Television programmes such as 'Dad's Army' have unfortunately associated the Home Guard with comedy, but in fact they performed much important work. The Guard posted sentries to watch for possible aircraft or parachute landings at likely spots such as disused aerodromes, golf courses on the outskirts of towns, local parks and racecourses. They manned anti-aircraft rocket guns, liaised with other units and with regular troops, set up communications and organised balloon barrages.

Other preparations were hastily made around the town. Place names and other identifying marks were obliterated to confuse the enemy about exactly where they were. Notices went up everywhere giving good advice to citizens on a number of issues. 'Keep Mum - she's not so dumb' warned people to take care what kind of information they passed on, as the person they were speaking to could be an enemy.

Older readers will remember how difficult it was to find certain items in the shops during the war; combs, soap, cosmetics, hairgrips, elastic, buttons, zips - all were virtually impossible to buy as factories that once produced these items had been turned over to war work. Stockings were in short supply, and resourceful women resorted to colouring their legs with gravy browning or with a mixture of sand and water. Beetroot juice was found to be a good substitute for lipstick.

Clothes rationing was introduced in 1941, and everyone had 66 coupons per year. Eleven coupons would buy a dress, and sixteen were needed for a coat. The number of coupons was later reduced to 40 per person. People were required to save material where they could - ladies' hemlines went up considerably, and skirts were not allowed to have lots of pleats. Some found clever ways around the regulations by using materials that were not rationed. Blackout material could be embroidered and made into blouses or skirts, and dyed sugar sacks were turned into curtains.

This smiling group was photographed outside the Vickers Armstrong dispersal factory at Shaw. Second from the left in the front row is Mary Griffin, nee Fry, and her story is perhaps typical of many young girls in wartime. Before the war Mary used to work in Woolworths in Northbrook Street. In 1940 she volunteered for war work, and spent much of the rest of the war drilling holes for air vents in aircraft components in the Vickers factory, where Spitfire sections were manufactured. All over the country, women like Mary were learning new skills, doing hard and sometimes dangerous jobs that had previously been regarded as men's work - and doing them well. In Newbury, essential war work also went on at Plenty's Eagle Ironworks, Newbury Diesel Company,

Opperman Gears Ltd from Islington and Elliotts' former furniture factory, converted to manufacture Horsa gliders and later Spitfire components and de Haviland fuselage. To release more Newbury women from their domestic duties, a nursery school was built in Victoria Park. Women were seen as such a vital labour force that later in the war even those aged 46 to 50 were required to register for war work; this, however, was not one of Mr Bevan's more popular measures. But there is no doubt that for many women enjoyed the experience of going out to work and shouldering new responsibilities; it changed their whole outlook on life, and they found it difficult to readjust to their traditional, more restricted role of home-maker when the war was over.

Above: War had been declared, and every citizen of Britain, young and old, male and female, was called upon to put his or her back into the war effort. Those who did not go into military service of one kind or another worked in factories, dug for victory, gave up their aluminium baths and saucepans, joined organisations and aided in any way they could. These boys were not going to be left out; they might be too young to fight but while there were sandbags to be filled they were going to do their bit to protect their school building. Thousands of sandbags were used during World War II to protect the country and its beautiful civic buildings.

Right: A proud father poses for the camera with his latest arrival. The baby had not arrived from Mars, in fact the 'arrival' was not a baby at all, but an anti-gas attack suit which was compulsory for babies in the United Kingdom during the second world war. An air pump at the side of the suit enabled anxious parents to replenish the supply of air to the precious package inside. It is said that most babies were less than enthusiastic abut the prospect of being encased in the suit - and who could blame them? The picture was taken in 1939. In the event there was never any gas attack on British soil during the course of the second world war.

The Spitfire did its bit in helping us win the war, so it is entirely fitting that this one should take its place in Newbury's victory celebrations, which began on 8th June 1946 and continued for three days. There was something for every age group. As well as the parades and processions, sports events were organised, a concert was held for the 'old folk', and Robert Morley's comedy Goodness How Sad was put on at the Plaza. At noon on the first day of the celebrations the Carnival Queen was crowned; that evening there was a torchlight procession along Parkway, with 1,000 torchbearers headed by Newbury Town Band, followed by a Victory Dance at the Corn Exchange which went on until midnight. On the Sunday there was a grand fireworks display. And throughout the celebrations everybody who bought a programme had a chance of winning a prize; each programme was numbered, and a lucky number might mean a cash prize, an ice-cream brick, a bottle of Brilliantine, a day out in a 6-seater chauffeured car to a destination of your choice - or a pound of tomatoes and a cucumber every week for a month.

The Ministry of Defence continued to maintain a high profile long after the end of the war; Exercise Discovery, seen here, took place in May 1953 and was an operation involving the Berkshire-based Food Flying Squad and the Civil Defence Experimental Mobile Column at Portsmouth. After the previous year's torrential rains which had brought serious flooding to the East Coast and claimed many lives in the Lynmouth disaster, people were only too conscious that catastrophic situations can arise in peacetime as well as in war; added to which, with the USAF at Greenham and the nation's fears of a nuclear war growing practically week by week - well, it was best to be prepared. On this photograph, taken at Victoria Barracks, Portsmouth, we see Miss

Events of the 1940s

HOT OFF THE PRESS

At the end of World War II in 1945 the Allies had their first sight of the unspeakable horrors of the Nazi extermination camps they had only heard of until then. In January, 4,000 emaciated prisoners more dead than alive were liberated by the Russians from Auschwitz in Poland, where three million people, most of them Jews, were murdered. The following year 23 prominent Nazis faced justice at Nuremberg; 12 of them were sentenced to death for crimes against humanity.

THE WORLD AT LARGE

The desert area of Alamogordo in New Mexico was the scene of the first atomic bomb detonation on July 16, 1945. With an explosive power equal to more than 15,000 tons of TNT, the flash could be seen 180 miles away. President Truman judged that the bomb could secure victory over Japan with far less loss of US lives than a conventional invasion, and on 6th August the first of the new weapons was dropped on Hiroshima. Around 80,000 people died.

ROYAL WATCH

By the end of World War II, the 19-year-old Princess Elizabeth and her distant cousin Lieutenant Philip Mountbatten RN were already in love. The King and Queen approved of Elizabeth's choice of husband, though they realised that she was rather young and had not mixed with many other young men. The engagement announcement was postponed until the Princess had spent four months on tour in Africa. The couple's wedding on 20th November 1947 was a glittering occasion - the first royal pageantry since before the war.

Neate, the Newbury WVS Centre Organiser, offering sandwiches to Portsmouth Civil Defence personnel. The WVS gave invaluable service during the war and continues to play a vital role to this day; during 1998 they provided 12 million meals on wheels to 100,000 recipients nationwide, and assisted at 128 actual emergencies. Her Majesty the Queen paid tribute to their work in 1966 by adding 'Royal' to their title.

JH Hole and HH Denness

Nowhere was safe during World War II . . . Newbury was potentially safer than many of Britain's towns and cities and so took in its share of evacuees, including 1,800 children from London - also the Lord Mayor of London's 'gold' coach, which was apparently evacuated to Newbury to keep it safe. Unfortunately the town did not completely escape the attentions of the enemy bomber. This scene of devastation is the aftermath of Newbury's worst air raid of the war. One Wednesday afternoon, 10th February 1943, a single plane appeared over Newtown Common and approached the town centre, flying low and dropping bombs. It followed a line which took it over Newtown Road cemetery, along Northbrook Street and then out towards Thatcham. Had the centre of Newbury been busier at the time there would have been more casualties, but as it was it left 15 people dead, many more injured, and a number of buildings in ruins. The photograph shows the wreckage of the St Bartholomew Almshouses. St John's Church was also destroyed, as was part of the senior school. Southampton Terrace was so badly damaged that it had to be completely demolished. A headstone was later erected in Shaw cemetery in memory of those killed.

At leisure

Below: The sight of so many happy smiles around the school dinner table might suggest that this isn't just another schoolday - not that the boys at Park House didn't always enjoy Mrs Martin's excellent school dinners, of course! But this is in fact a special occasion; they are having Christmas dinner, and many of them are too intent on eating - or, in one case, getting the last drop of gravy out of the jug - even to pull faces at the camera. Anyone who regularly had school dinners will find the dining arrangements imprinted indelibly on their memory; at Park House, the Assembly Hall doubled as dining hall and boys sat eight to a table, with one prefect per table who designated two monitors to fetch the trays from the kitchen, and who was then responsible for dishing out the food - which of course consisted of a main course and a pud, with plenty of good old-fashioned stodge, just what growing boys needed. In

the post-war era Park House took boys aged between 11 and 15; Park House itself, purchased for a sum of around £7,000 to house the school following the destruction of its former premises during the war, was extended in the 1950s to ease the overcrowding. We are told that the Headmaster at the time of this photograph was Mr Turnbull.

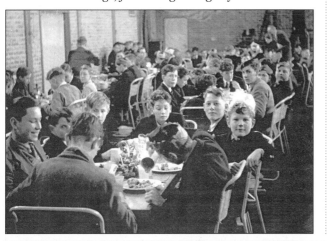

Bottom: The Corn Exchange, traditionally the place where farmers sold their grain, has been the venue for all manner of different events over the years: political meetings, concerts, plays, opera, exhibitions, dinners, dances, hunt balls, discos, ice skating, roller skating, films - and, as we see on this photograph, wrestling. The referee's flares suggest that this particular contest took place in the 60s, and indeed wrestling enjoyed widespread popularity in the mid-60s to 70s, with commentator Kent Walton presenting a regular Saturday afternoon all-in wrestling slot on ITV. Wrestling matches had been held in the Corn Exchange during the war, with local wrestler Jack Curtis among those featured. However, when wrestling promoters in London applied in 1959 for permission to hold fixtures there on a regular basis, a lengthy debate ensued. Some town councillors took the view that wrestling was not a suitable spectacle for the people of the town and, what was more, would attract undesirables to Newbury. Others thought it was not for the Town Council to censor what the public could watch. In the end the latter view prevailed; and the packed seats do suggest that in fact people had no objection whatsoever to watching wrestling. The crowd looks meek enough, too - any undesirables present have tactfully kept out of the way of the photographer.

Surrounded by the noise of merry crowds and fairground music, the smell of toffee and the steam of the traction engines, surely even a statue must warm to the occasion! The Michaelmas Fair has been enjoyed by many, many generations in Newbury. Originally it had a serious purpose: for more than a century it was a hiring fair, where those looking for work would assemble in Market Place on the first Thursday after Michaelmas Day, tradi-

tionally wearing a symbol of their trade - for instance, an agricultural worker might pin an ear of corn to his clothes - in the hopes of attracting the attention of a prospective employer. By the 20th century this practice had been dropped and the fair had become purely an annual entertainment, giving people a final opportunity to enjoy outdoor festivities before winter arrived. Filling the market place and stretching down to the Wharf, lit by lantern and

with every kind of sideshow imaginable - fat ladies, fortune tellers, roundabouts, toffee stalls, even 'a ferocious dragon from Wild Wales' - the Fair turned the whole of the town centre into a place of fun and revelry, as we see on this photograph. The presence of Queen Victoria indicates that this scene must have been captured before 1933. The Fair was banished to Northcroft in 1945 as it was considered too disruptive for the town centre, and apparently traction engines remain banned from Market Place to this day.

Events of the 1940s

MELODY MAKERS
The songs of radio personalities such as Bing Crosby and Vera Lynn were whistled, sung and hummed everywhere during the 1940s. The 'forces' sweetheart' brought hope to war-torn Britain with 'When the Lights go on Again', while the popular crooner's 'White Christmas' is still played around Christmas time even today. Who can forget songs like 'People Will Say we're in Love', 'Don't Fence Me In', 'Zip-a-dee-doo-dah', and 'Riders in the Sky'?

INVENTION AND TECHNOLOGY
Inspired by quick-drying printers' ink, in 1945 Hungarian journalist Laszlo Biro developed a ballpoint pen which released viscous ink from its own reservoir as the writer moved the pen across the page. An American inventor was working on a similar idea at the same time, but it was Biro's name that stuck. A few years later Baron Bich developed a low cost version of the pen, and the 'Bic' ballpoint went on sale in France in 1953.

SCIENCE AND DISCOVERY
In 1943 Ukrainian-born biochemist Selman Abraham Waksman made a significant discovery. While studying organisms found in soil he discovered an antibiotic (a name Waksman himself coined) which was later found to be the very first effective treatment for tuberculosis. A major killer for thousands of years, even the writings of the ancient Egyptians contain stories of people suffering from tuberculosis. Waksman's development of streptomycin brought him the 1952 Nobel Prize for Medicine.

Above: These charming cottages, with their dusting of snow, make a perfect Christmas card scene. Sadly they are no longer there; this land was acquired by the hospital, and the cottages, which stood on the corner of Hampton Road and Rectory Close, were demolished shortly after the photograph was taken. Around this spot lies the City, an interesting area which has changed a great deal over the years. Throughout most of the 19th century it was a notoriously poor place; its residents felt obliged to look after their own interests in order to survive, which earned them something of a bad reputation with the rest of the town. Very much a separate community, the City even used to have its own annually-elected Mayor - who wore a cocked hat and chain of office older than those belonging to Newbury Corporation. Towards the end of the 19th century improvements were carried out, and it gradually turned into the very pleasant area which it is today.

Right: Railways used to exercise the same fascination over the average small boy as do virtual reality spaceships these days. What better way to spend a wet Sunday than working out a new layout for your Hornby set? And on a nice day, the miniature railway at Penwood was a very popular attraction for children from all over Newbury - as can be seen from the boys' craning necks and eager faces, with not an empty seat visible as the train rounds the bend and crosses the little bridge on this snapshot from 1953. Begun as one man's hobby, the railway then started to give rides to the public, and for many Newbury families an expedition to Penwood became a favourite weekend treat. One imagines that children born into the third millennium and surrounded from birth by push-button hi-tec entertainment may begin to wonder what on earth their predecessors used to do, in the dim and distant days before computers and even television were invented; well, they used to have fun, is the answer!

Events of the 1950s

WHAT'S ON?
Television hit Britain in a big way during the 1950s. Older readers will surely remember 'Double Your Money, Dixon of Dock Green and 'Dragnet' (whose characters' names were changed 'to protect the innocent'). Commercial television was introduced on 22nd September 1955, and Gibbs SR toothpaste were drawn out of the hat to become the first advert to be shown. Many believed adverts to be vulgar, however, and audiences were far less than had been hoped for.

GETTING AROUND
The year 1959 saw the development of the world's first practical air-cushion vehicle - better known to us as the hovercraft. The earliest model was only able to travel at slow speeds over very calm water and was unable to carry more than three passengers. The faster and smoother alternative to the sea ferry quickly caught on, and by the 1970s a 170-ton car-carrying hovercraft service had been introduced across the English Channel.

SPORTING CHANCE
The four-minute mile had remained the record since 1945, and had become regarded as virtually unbreakable. On 6th May 1954, however, Oxford University student Roger Bannister literally ran away with the record, accomplishing the seemingly impossible in three minutes 59.4 seconds. Bannister collapsed at the end of his last amazing lap, even temporarily losing his vision. By the end of the day, however, he had recovered sufficiently to celebrate his achievement in a London night club!

It didn't much matter if you hadn't got a shop-bought tricycle - you could have just as much fun with a home-made bogey! This photograph was taken in Pembroke Road in 1959, when little chaps like these could still trundle up and down safely and enjoy all the thrills and spills of a happy, carefree childhood - albeit under the watchful eye of all the mothers in the street. These days the notion of growing up in Pembroke Road, with its

impersonal offices and car parks, seems a trifle bizarre, but in the first half of the century this was an area where families lived and worked and raised their families, and the street would have buzzed with life. There were plenty of passers-by, too: folk cutting through on their way from one part of town to another, as well as those attending functions at the

Northbrook meeting rooms or going to the squash club at 9 Pembroke Road. When the squash club became a hostel and canteen for the US troops during the second world war, Pembroke Road must have turned into a veritable hive of activity, ringing with the footsteps and voices of our Allies, and would certainly have been a lively place to live!

The families in the business of keeping good things in store for Newbury

It is no exaggeration to say that Newbury would not be the same without Camp Hopson. Camp Hopson's Department Store is generally regarded as the core of the town's shopping centre today, as it has been for more than three-quarters of a century, but we should not forget that the influence of the two families who amalgamated their business interests in 1921 extends back far beyond this date, to the mid 19th century, and the activities of successive generations of the families, many of whom were leading and highly-respected public figures, have made a great contribution to civic and cultural life in Newbury.

One intriguing legacy from the very early days of the Hopson family business takes the form of photographic portraits of some of the townsfolk of the 1850s, taken by Joseph Hopson. Joseph was a professional photographer, and was in fact the first commercial photographer in Newbury; he also offered his services as a decorator and paper-hanger. His original business premises, which he occupied from 1851 onwards, were at 64 Northbrook Street, and around a decade later he also took the adjoining premises at the corner of Northbrook Street and West Street, where he established himself in the furniture trade. The family firm

was to remain on this site until 1921; Joseph's sons Joseph (Jnr) and Frederic both joined the business, and carried it on after their father's death in 1899.

Like their father, both brothers played active roles in public life - a tradition which has been preserved through subsequent generations of the family to the present day. Joseph (Snr) had served as a town councillor between 1878 and 1897, when he was elected Alderman of the Borough; his numerous other public appointments included that of Mayor in 1882, and he was a Sunday School teacher at the Congregational Church for 60 years. This latter connection was continued by both his sons, with Joseph acting as organist and Sunday School teacher for 50 years, and Frederic as Church secretary, deacon, Sunday School superintendent and school secretary. Frederic played a leading role in public life, serving as Councillor, Mayor, Alderman and JP and doing a great deal to help those in need. Joseph meanwhile was one of the town's most successful gardeners, a talented photographer and a keen bird-watcher, but his

Above: *An invoice dating from 1921.*
Below: *The original Hopson premises on Northbrook Street c1870.*

come to Newbury in 1886 to take over the drapery firm of Bodman & Jones, at 8-10 Northbrook Street. Alfred Camp's progressive ideas gave a new lease of life to what had previously been a rather old-fashioned business, transforming it into the Drapery Bazaar. Within ten years he had absorbed a neighbouring drapery concern, Messrs Payne & Vince, which he turned into a Men's Outfitting Department. His wife Mim, whom he married around 1885, also became involved in the business, as did Herbert, their second son, who was apparently an accomplished snooker player and an amateur 'cellist. Shortly afterwards the announcement of an amalgamation between the Drapery Bazaar and Hopson's caused great excitement in Newbury.

By May, 1921 Messrs Camp Hopson & Co Limited was established in a whole row of shops stretching from 6 to 14 Northbrook Street. As the Newbury Weekly News put it, 'Such an undertaking marks a new chapter of commercial enterprise in the business life of the town.' Both the Drapery Bazaar and Hopson & Sons had earned excellent reputations for their high standards, and the new establishment lived up to expectations. It carried an extremely wide range of merchandise, and at the same time it took care to preserve the personal service to customers - two qualities which are still appreciated by the people of Newbury today.

greatest interest was music. He was a fine bassoonist, and over a period of 50 years he played in every concert given by the Newbury Amateur Orchestral Union. Regarded by his contemporaries as the 'father' of this NAOU, orchestral standards in the town were raised considerably as a result of his efforts.

In the hands of the founder's two sons, Hopson & Sons continued to prosper. In due course Joseph's son Paul entered the family business, after spending time in France during the war as a lorry-driver with the RASC; and in 1920 he married Miss Norah Camp. Miss Camp was the daughter of Mr Alfred Camp, a Devonshire businessman who had

Above left: *The interior of the Northbrook Street store in 1921.* ***Top:*** *Queen Victoria 1887 celebrations - Hopson & Sons, 64 Northbrook Street.*

The company's vehicles became a regular feature on the streets of Newbury. Up until the late 1920s deliveries and removals were effected using horse-drawn pantechnicons and lift-vans. These were then abandoned in favour of a motorised transport fleet which included a 4 ton Dennis and a 30 cwt Dennis, both fitted with Luton bodies, a 12 cwt Morris van, a 7 cwt Austin van, and a four-tonner which could be used to pull a covered Carrimore trailer. The company ran all its vehicles on BP No 1 petrol, insisted on using only the highest quality lubricants, and was apparently very pleased when it discovered how low the repair and maintenance costs for the new fleet were (how times change!). Meanwhile the last of their old pantechnicons was ingeniously converted into a very comfortable caravan.

Following the formation of Camp Hopson in 1920, Herbert Camp and Paul Hopson became junior directors; the original board of directors also included John Ward, who had been a manager at the Drapery bazaar since 1897 and was related to the Camp family through his marriage

Above: An early Dennis van used by Camp Hopson Removals. Below: A 1937 delivery van.

to Alfred Camp's niece Mary Evelyn Rice; and Bernard de Castro - better known as Bill - also became a director in 1924. Bill Castro had been with Camp Hopson for some years, and took responsibility for the removals, funeral and contracts side of the Camp Hopson business.

During the 30s the company, already established as the largest retailer in the town and employing a staff of around 150, hit upon the novel idea of using their fleet of commercial vehicles for advertising. They had a different picture painted on each side of each of their four vans, at a total cost of £129.12s.6d. Each of these eight pictures advertised a particular department - hosiery and fashion, sportswear, furniture and furnishings, outfitting, millinery, building and decorating, and removals and warehousing, the latter appearing on both the pantechnicons. Another surprisingly modern idea which the company had was to reserve the registration numbers 590, 591 and 592, these being the same as its telephone numbers.

All too soon, however, such pleasant matters as settling upon the livery of the vans were overshadowed by the war. A few years before the outbreak of hostilities John Ward died at the age of only 59. Like Joseph Hopson Junior, John had been a music-lover; a member of Newbury Choral Society for many years, he was remembered for his fine bass voice. Sadly, his death came just a few months after he became Chairman of Camp Hopson. This position was then taken over by Bert Camp, who guided the company through the war years. The imposition of rationing and clothing coupons brought the growth of the business to a temporary halt, with many of the staff away in the armed forces. Mrs Camp put in extra hours to keep the accounts up to date, while the building division constructed pill boxes along the Kennet and Avon canal and undertook structural repairs after the air raid on Newbury in 1943. Just as trade was beginning to recover in the aftermath of

the war, it suffered another blow in the form of the death of Bert Camp in December 1948.

Paul Hopson took over as Chairman, and over the next two decades a great deal of modernisation was carried out at the store. Structural alterations to the premises had to be carried out with extreme care because of the age of the property, but these constructional problems were overcome successfully and by the end of the 60s an additional floor area of more than 15,000 square feet had been created. An extension to the rear of the ground floor provided a larger display area for furniture, which remained one of the most important parts of the business, and new departments including cosmetics, china and glass. Expansion continued, and the 1970s saw the company established as one of the largest independent stores between London, Bristol and Southampton. Five hundred people attended the Fashion Show and champagne reception held in 1971, the year of the company's 50th anniversary, to

mark the opening of the new fashion floor, and Camp Hopson donated the proceeds of the reception, which amounted to more than £2,500, to the Duchess of Roxburgh as President of the National Society for Cancer Relief. The following year's projects included an escalator - the first in Newbury - and the Penthouse restaurant; further extensions followed, and a new £40,000 NCR computer was installed on the second floor in 1978. By 1981 the 60-year old store was employing more than 225 people, and its administration offices and Board Room had moved to a restored Georgian cottage. This cottage was formerly owned by the Camp family, and following a complete programme of internal and external renovation by the company it became a very attractive feature in a much-changed part of Newbury.

Recent developments at the Camp Hopson store will be fresh in the minds of most readers. Suffice it to say that the company has maintained throughout its policy of providing a personal service and recognising the importance of the individual, while continuing to evolve along the same dynamic, forward-looking and innovative lines that brought it such great success over almost 80 years. The company has remained a family business in every sense of the term; the current Chairman is David Hopson, who took on the post at the age of only 37, having joined the business in 1953 and been appointed a director in 1961. The current generation's commitment to the town which has been home to both branches of the family remains as strong as ever. Sue, his wife, is well-known to many for her work in collecting photographs, recording local history and ensuring that the town's heritage is preserved for posterity.

Above: A 1967 sale.
Top: A Camp Hopson float from 1951.
Right: The fashion department in 1981.

Memories of NEWBURY

The Present
The Camp Hopson group today consists of four main operating divisions:

1. The Department Store: With over 30 departments, and an acre of selling space, Camp Hopson's refurbished department store offers a unique selection of quality brand names at value for money prices.

2. The Furniture Centre: Launched in April 1998, the Furniture Centre in Park Way, Newbury, offers the latest ranges in quality furniture, beds, carpets and soft furnishings. There is also the 'Upper Deck' coffee shop, overlooking the Kennet and Avon Canal.

The Furniture Centre and Department Store are both covered by Camp Hopson's 'Price Match Guarantee' - the customer's guarantee of unbeatable value, and there are over 100 car parking spaces available for both stores.

3. Camp Hopson Removals: Based in Hambridge Lane, Newbury, Camp Hopson Removals' fully trained staff operate a modern fleet of removal vehicles and a complete range of containerised storage facilities. The Company specialises in domestic removals and has also recently set up a weekly delivery service to London.

Above left: *David Hopson, Chairman, Camp Hopson.*
Below: *One of the company's new removal lorries.*
Bottom: *Camp Hopson Department Store, Northbrook Street.*

4. Camp Hopson Funerals: Camp Hopson Funerals recently re-located to West Street, Newbury, and continues to offer a personal, caring and professional service, from re-furbished premises, which were originally built by Joseph Hopson & Sons in 1905.

A common factor throughout all Camp Hopson is the level of care and personal attention shown to customers, and in this respect, the company is well-served by its complement of over 250 staff; many of whom have worked with the company for over 25 years.

In recognition of the loyalty of staff and customers alike, Camp Hopson is proud to have reached the finals of Drapers Record 'Department Store of the Year Award' for both 1998 and 1999 - the judging for this year's award is still continuing as this book goes to press!

The Future
Newbury, with its unique market town heritage and wide range of different shopping, leisure and cultural attractions, is currently well-placed to successfully compete against its regional neighbours such as Reading, Basingstoke, Swindon and Oxford.

Initiating and managing change continues to increase in importance for businesses, and Camp Hopson will, no doubt, continue to play its part in helping Newbury to thrive in future.

Left: *Des Guthrie, Managing Director, Camp Hopson.*
Below: *Camp Hopson Funerals, West Street.*
Bottom: *Camp Hopson Furniture Centre, Park Way.*

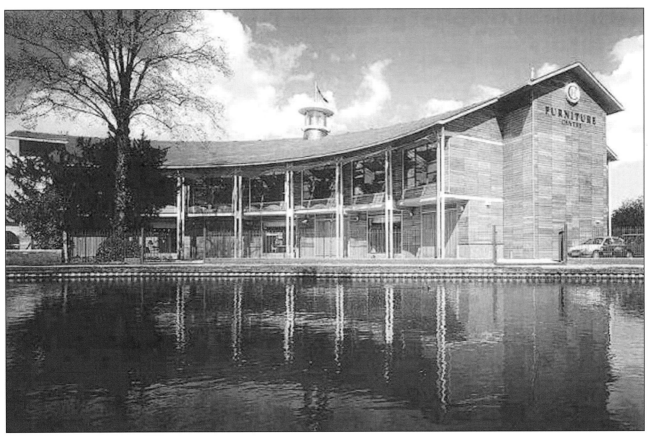

Not just castles in the air

Newbury Building Society, established in 1856 by a group of local business men, uses as its proud slogan, 'Where castles in the air take shape' and making local people's home owning dreams come true - giving those castles in the air some substance - is exactly what this Building Society hopes to achieve. An important aspect of the Building Society is its emphasis on the local side of its business. There is strong loyalty at the Society to the local area, the local history, the local people and their needs. In keeping with this, the move back to the Society's original 'home' in Northbrook Street in 1993 was celebrated with a 'Back to Northbrook Street...' booklet. But before moving back to Northbrook Street, let's look at the long road one of the oldest Building Societies in Britain has travelled on its highly successful journey.

Most successful companies start from small beginnings, and the fledgling Newbury Permanent Benefit Building and Investment Society, as it was originally named, was no exception. On October 8th at number 62 Northbrook Street, Newbury, several local worthies, including two previous Newbury Mayors - John H Mason and Joseph F Hickman - and members of families still well known and respected in the area today, met in the offices of solicitor Frederick Talbot.

They chose to form the Society as a permanent building society rather than the more usual (at the time) terminating society. The founders had immediately shown the independence of thought which would stand them in good stead in later years and which would lead to this particular Building Society still being independent a good century and a half later. The very first share certificate was made out to John Mason himself on the fifth of

Above left: *Northbrook Street at the end of the nineteenth century.*
Above right: *Newbury Weekly News 1901.*
Below: *Bartholomew Street.*
Bottom: *The first share certificate.*

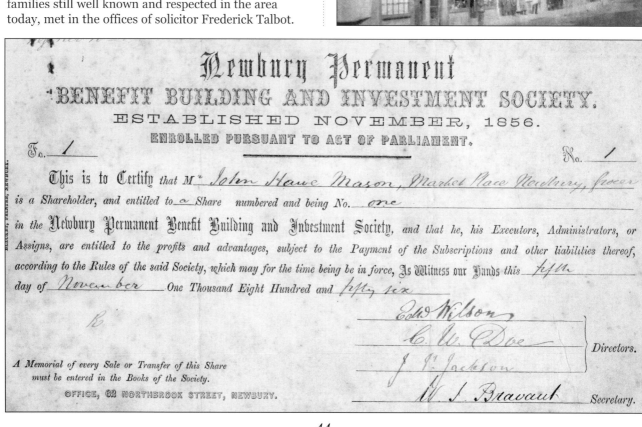

November that same year, witnessed by his fellow directors and the Society Secretary, Mr W Bravant. Business was immediately put on a formal footing, with two directors deputed to attend each month to receive members' subscriptions, their remuneration for this being the princely sum of 2/6.

It wasn't all plain sailing unfortunately and the first borrower proved himself untrustworthy and fell into arrears. Legal steps had to be taken to ensure payment of the necessary contributions. Total profit for the first year was just fourteen pounds and ten shillings. The total number of members was at the time 57. It would be true to say that the Society has grown somewhat since, but more of that later...for the time being, the first company Annual General Meeting reported mortgage advances of £840. The business, though small, was truly underway.

At the beginning of 1894, the re-named Newbury Permanent Benefit Building Society, in need of an injection of funds, took over the Newbury and District Industrial Building Society, thus benefiting both Societies and their members. Whilst the 'Permanent' was more than happy to accept the influx of cash which the merger brought, the 'District' was also at the time sorely in need of the 'Permanent's' more successful

management skills. At this time the position of solicitor to the Society was taken on by Mr W H Belcher, marking a relationship with the Society which has remained firm right through to the present day. Interestingly, in 1989, Louch Belcher and Co, solicitors, merged with Charles Lucas and Marshall, who then became the Society's solicitors, regaining the position lost when Charles Lucas resigned the post, making way for Mr Belcher, way back in 1894.

Now perhaps feeling more confident of their position, in 1896, the directors arranged for the purchase of premises in Northbrook Street, for the sum of £525. Operations continued to be run from Northbrook Street until the 1930s when new premises were acquired at 19

Above left: The company premises in the early 1900s.
Top: 17-20 Bartholomew Street.
Below: Liddiards the butchers on Northbrook Street in the nineteenth century.

Bartholomew Street. Over the years adjoining properties were added to increase the Society's working area - including the old dairy to the rear of the buildings - until finally in 1982, with no more suitable properties to annex, the Society built its new Head Quarters on the site of the now burnt-down dairy. Perhaps inevitably, this Headquarters building also has since been extended several times - probably neither staff nor members are complaining of the need for that!

Back in the late 1880s and early 1900s the Society continued to flourish. In 1906 assets of £50,000 were recorded. By 1932 this had increased tenfold to £500,000 and the Society changed its name once more, this time to the more economically-worded Newbury Bulding Society. A time of great vision and change, it was at this point that an important figure in the Society's history was appointed - as a lowly clerk. Mr John Green, later to be, in turn, Secretary, General Manager and finally Director, is credited with building up the Society's branch network during the 1970s. It's not clear whether his new employers recognised his potential from the beginning however and back in 1933 he was concerned with more mundane tasks than developing company strategy - he recalls his first duty as buying a packet of paper clips from the shop across the road! Mr Green retired from the Board in 1987, having served the Society loyally for 55 years, interrupted only by the war.

The war didn't only interrupt the service of Mr Green however. In common with most other businesses at the time (the Fifty Shilling Tailors were advertising in the local paper during the war years, encour-

aging people not to buy unless essential) the Society put business on hold for the duration. The Building Societies Association, of which Newbury Building Society was a member, recommended in 1939 that mortgage advances be suspended 'for the present'. With the enforced absence of menfolk both as staff and members it's safe to assume the war years, as for most businesses, were not a high point.

In 1935 the Society had moved to offices in Bartholomew Street to cater for the population growth taking place in the south of Newbury and at the end of hostilities developments continued apace. In 1946 the first passbooks were issued to members. Transactions were manually recorded - a time-consuming job - but this was a considerably simpler method of record keeping than that it replaced - the

Below and bottom: *Northbrook Street scenes at the turn of the twentieth century.*

issue of share certificates to the value of £10 and £25 to record transactions. Assets broke the magic £1 million mark for the first time.

In 1962, with home ownership booming and a wealth of steady jobs available for an increasingly affluent population, the first branch outside Newbury was opened, in Aldershot. Further branches followed in the 1970s and 1980s, in small market towns in the surrounding area, the success of these branches being largely credited for the continually increasing financial strength of the Society. It is also a fact worth mentioning that many of the company's notable staff have, like John Green, stayed with the Society for a very long period of employment. By way of example, the Society has employed only eight Company Secretaries in the whole of its 143 year history, including the first one, William Bravant, who worked for 35 years in the position and Sid Povey who was Secretary for 22 years. The loyalty which the Society has shown to the local people has been repaid by the loyalty of strong capable employees and managers who have between them made the Society a great success.

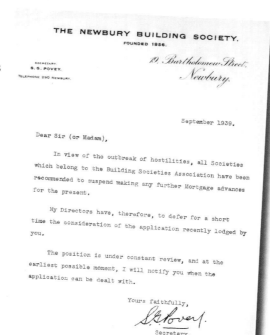

THE NEWBURY BUILDING SOCIETY.
FOUNDED 1856.

SECRETARY.
S. G. POVEY.
TELEPHONE 290 NEWBURY.

19. *Bartholomew Street*,
Newbury.

September 1939.

Dear Sir (or Madam),

In view of the outbreak of hostilities, all Societies which belong to the Building Societies Association have been recommended to suspend making any further Mortgage advances for the present.

My Directors have, therefore, to defer for a short time the consideration of the application recently lodged by you.

The position is under constant review, and at the earliest possible moment, I will notify you when the application can be dealt with.

Yours faithfully,

S G Povey.

Secretary.

In the late 1960s the Society's accounting and bookkeeping records were transferred into computer format and in 1974 Newbury Building Society took another major leap forward with the introduction of an IBM computer system in Head Office. The branch network followed the computer trail in the early 1980s, with the introduction of a state-of-the-art processing system. There's a wicked rumour that a certain Mr Fleming, then a young accountant, but later appointed Chief Executive in 1992, forgot that first computerised morning to switch the power on to the system - but it's probably not true! New systems followed to keep the Society at the cutting edge of technology. Handwritten transactions are now just a hazy memory in the company's history - indeed, with assets reaching £200 million in 1992, and over £340 million in 1999, it's hard to see how the Society could possibly function without the help of its considerable electronic technology.

A major step in the Society's recent history, and one which seems to have engendered a nostalgic response in

Above: *A letter dating from 1939 which was beginning to deal with the effects of the ensuing war.*
Top: *Northbrook Street from the bridge in the 1930s.*

employees and townspeople alike, was the move back to Northbrook Street in 1993. Whilst the Head Office remains in the new Bartholomew Street building (although the original offices were sold) a branch was opened in Northbrook Street at number 105B, also known as Bridge House. The move had a sentimental appeal for the Society, a representation of going back to its roots for an organisation which has been true to its original purposes and intentions. Always a local company, the Building Society has itself shown an interest in the history of the building and the area, filling its brochure to mark the opening of the new branch with snippets of information and photographs.

Newbury was founded by a Norman lord, Arnulf de Hesdin, where the Winchester-Oxford road crossed the Kennet. Over the centuries, Newbury's Northbrook Street, connecting the settlement to the south of the Kennet with the Roman road system which ran from Cirencester to Silchester, has had its significant periods. Jack of Newbury, owner of the first factory in England, sited that factory in Northbrook Street and on account of his great industry was chosen to meet Henry VIII and Catherine of Aragon on their 1518 visit to the area. In 1623 the original wooden bridge collapsed, possibly due to the weight of the buildings built on it. By 1767 a total of 1176 people were recorded as living in Northbrook Street, probably crammed in owing to the local planning system of building 'double sets' of houses. In 1769 work began on the new bridge, designed by James Clarke and still in use today. In 1810 the canal was opened to London-Bristol traffic. As a result, underneath the Society's branch there are deep grooves caused by the hauling lines for the barges. Later in the century, on the occasion of Queen

Victoria's accession, a celebratory procession was held in Northbrook Street.

The building which serves as the Society's latest branch, adjoining the Water Bridge which is of such importance to the town, has itself had a variety of previous uses, although bookselling has featured prominently, from as far back in time as William Roe who sold books and stationery alongside his printing work in 1844, right up to

Above: *The Northbrook Street premises today.*
Top: *One of the Building Society's advertising campaigns.*

the 1970s when the building had been for some time a branch of the rather more famous W H Smith. A sign of how seriously the Society regards its local responsibilities is the fact that it has included the bridge shelter at 105B as part of its programme of restoration. This is in addition to the restoration work already undertaken on the building itself - now 'restored to its Georgian splendour' in the words of former Chairman of the Society, David Hopson.

There is no doubt about the pride with which the Society regards its position on this busy and historically significant street, and the care they intend to take of both the building and its immediate surroundings.

Anyone who has been to Newbury will have taken note of the high profile the Society enjoys within the town. There are eye-catching Newbury Building Society decorated buses to been seen wending their way through the shopping areas: there is a Newbury Building Society Balloon Team offering high-flying advertising opportu-

nities on balloons and trailers alike; there is sponsorship of local events such as the Newbury Show and significant support of local charities including the hospital, housing associations and the arts.

But all this would be in vain without the basics of what clients require from a Building Society - financial benefits and good value for money. In 1999 mortgage advances from the Newbury Building Society exceeded £70 million. Over 100 well trained staff were employed. Membership exceeded 45,000 throughout the Thames Valley. The Society remains committed to both independence and the provision of a high quality service for members, including the lowest possible mortgage rates. A wide variety of financial services are available, expanding constantly to keep abreast of current customer requirements.

Newbury Building Society has shown its commitment to the area and its affection for the people of Newbury by its longstanding employment of local staff. With the opening of the Northbrook Street branch back in 1993

local people were encouraged to pay a visit not only to transact business but also to learn more about the grand building, to admire the restoration, enjoy the view and to take pride, alongside the Society, in what had been achieved. If the Society is pleased with its progress then it has every right to be - from those small beginnings in 1856 has grown a truly independent Building Society committed to the best deal for its local members. A Society clear-sighted enough to look to the future whilst also public-spirited enough to take care of the past it shares with its hometown.

Left and below: *The Newbury Building Society Balloon Team in action.*

Events & occasion

Another long-established Newbury tradition - the Boxing Day Meet. The Craven Hunt - now the Vine Craven, following a merger in the 1960s - draws huge crowds to Market Place every year to see the colourful and impressive spectacle. Even those who have little involvement in country sports throughout the year come along to see the glossy, immaculately-groomed horses and their smartly turned out riders, the gleaming tack, and the fit, well-trained hounds; while for those taking part, the meet is a prelude to what may well turn out to be a long and exhausting but thrilling day out. The date of this particular photograph is uncertain, but the presence of the motor coach suggests that it is post-war. Whatever the date, we are fairly safe in assuming that a certain Frank Neate was among those preparing to follow the hunt, as a newspaper report of 1959 accorded him the distinction of being the only supporter who had ridden to the Craven pack ever since the turn of the century.

Left: The absence of smoke in the air, and the calm, cheerful air of those involved suggest that this is a practice, rather than an actual fire. The date is believed to be the early 30s, by which time Newbury Fire Brigade boasted two motorised vehicles, though neither is in evidence here. The Volunteer Fire Brigade was set up in 1879; its fire station on the wharf housed a steam fire engine, bought new for £600, and Newbury Volunteer Brigade, with its own distinctive buttons and heavy brass helmets, was a welcome and reassuring presence in the town until the second world war. The National Fire Services Authority then took over all the local brigades, and after the war the fire service was reorganised, with responsibility for firefighting in the area going to Berkshire County Council in 1956. The fire station, which during the war had sounded the air raid warning siren from its tower, was then demolished. Notorious fires in Newbury over the years include the one at the New Brothers Mill in Bartholomew Street in 1937, the one at Carlton Cinema in Cheap Street in the early hours of Bank Holiday Monday in 1950, possibly started by a burning cigarette end dropped by a member of the Sunday night audience, the one which gutted the House of Toomer in Northbrook Street in April 1961 and the infamous fire which destroyed Lock Cottage, whose cause was never satisfactorily determined.

Below: These days we have learned to be more discreet about unemployment; the size of the problem can be deduced from the figures that are issued, but we no longer see queues stretching from the Labour Exchange to West Mills, as we did in the early 30s. The severity of the situation in 1932 was such that a Vigilance Committee was formed, and a deputation to the Council was planned. The Council responded to the situation first by offering allotments, which did not help a great deal, and then by launching Newbury Work Fund Scheme, which did; and to celebrate the scheme, a mass meeting was held in the Corn Exchange, with a procession headed by Newbury Town Silver Band, followed by a concert in Market Place. The scheme was of immense benefit both to those whom it employed and to the town; a new road - Parkway - was built, and ambitious plans for improving the facilities at Victoria Park were carried out, including the creation of a boating lake, paddling pool, bowling green, tennis courts and Pavilion. Incidentally, the fire engine seen at the head of this procession, PG 3076, was the Voluntary Fire Brigade's second motorised vehicle, purchased in 1930.

Bottom: Looking across a sea of hats - in 1933, you wore your hat when you went out, and if you were a woman you kept it on until you got home again - we can see assembled on stage, behind Mayor Kimber, the children who are taking part in the annual music festival in the Corn Exchange. While the Mayor addresses the audience, no doubt all the proud mums are keeping an anxious eye on their offspring to make sure that their hair has stayed tidy and they are not fidgeting. The Mayor's speech was likely to be lively; Elsie Kimber, the first woman mayor of Newbury, was certainly a character. The daughter of a local shopkeeper, Elsie began making herself useful at an early age, going out in the horse and trap to collect orders from the customers; and once the orders had been packed she would be back to deliver them, accompanied by an older assistant. The Kimbers' shop was a high-class grocer - we would probably call it a delicatessen - stocking a good range of quality goods including cheeses and spices, and selling nothing prepackaged except butter, flour and sugar. Elsie, who never married, grew up to be an excellent businesswoman, and was the first woman President of the Grocers' Association before becoming Mayor of Newbury in 1932.

Right: Throughout the 20th century Newbury Racecourse formed the arena not only for many great dramas not only in the world of racing, but in the world at large as well. Under military occupation in the first world war, the racecourse served purposes as diverse as a hay dispersal centre and (as again

in WW2) a prisoner of war camp. Racing was resumed in 1919 but the site was requisitioned again upon the outbreak of World War II, to be occupied successively by the Berkshire Yeomanry, the Oxford & Bucks Light Infantry, the Lancashire Fusiliers and the Royal Fusiliers. This photograph shows a ceremonial parade taking place on the racecourse in 1940, complete with armoured personnel carriers and infantrymen in gas masks. But racing went on even with areas turned over to military purposes, and was not completely abandoned until the site was handed over to the Americans. It became their G45 Supply Depot, then the 9th Main Supply Depot RASC; and by the time the allies had laid concrete roads and some 35 miles of railway lines, racing really was out of the question. Re-turfing and rebuilding work began after the end of the war and continued for many years.

Newbury has turned out to pay its last respects to three gallant firemen - one aged 41, another 37, and the youngest just 28 - who were tragically killed by enemy action during the second world war. On the day they met their deaths, the three men had all been engaged in firefighting in the Midlands, but when a massive air raid was launched over Portsmouth they were sent there to assist in bringing under control the numerous blazes started by the bombs. The blitz continued, and the three men died when the naval dockyard where they were fighting a fire was hit by a bomb. Not only relatives and colleagues but the whole of Newbury was stunned by the tragedy. The three were buried at Newbury Parish Church on 14th March 1941, and the funeral procession is seen here making its way along a Northbrook Street lined by mourners. On 9th March 1949 a ceremony was held at the fire station and a plaque to their memory was unveiled. The 50th anniversary of the tragedy was commemorated by the dedication of a bronze memorial near St Paul's Church in London. Their bravery will never be forgotten by the people of Newbury.

Everything stops for tea - except this Hovis lorry, which keeps moving, bringing a smile to the faces of partakers and observers alike. The date is 8th June 1951, and the occasion was Newbury's Festival of Britain celebrations. Britain had put the war behind it and was looking forward to the future with enthusiasm, and Newbury was putting on a fine show. All the traditional popular events and entertainments were included in the Festival - cabaret, dances, folk dancing, a horticultural show, and all kind of competitive sports from motorcycle grass track racing, to bowling, to darts, all presided over by a gorgeous Festival Queen. In addition, the shops were

encouraged to put on a good window display, with a prize on offer for the best. So Newbury was a merry and colourful place to be; and that, of course, was an important aspect of the Festival - to create a mood of optimism and confidence all over Britain. The proceeds of Newbury's merrymaking on this occasion were used for the elderly, with funds raised being put into restoring the almshouses.

Events of the 1950s

HOT OFF THE PRESS
The 1950s seemed to be the heyday of spies, and in 1951 the activities of Guy Burgess and Donald Maclean caused a sensation in the country. Both had occupied prominent positions in the Foreign Office, while Burgess had also been a member of MI-6. Recruited by the Russians while at Cambridge University in the 1930s, the traitors provided the Soviets with a huge amount of valuable information. They disappeared in 1951, surfacing in Moscow five years later.

THE WORLD AT LARGE
Plans to develop the economies of member states into one common market came to fruition on 1st January 1958, when the EEC came into operation. The original members were France, Belgium, Luxembourg, The Netherlands, Italy, and West Germany. The Community became highly successful, achieving increased trade and prosperity across Western Europe while at the same time alleviating fear of war which lingered on after the end of World War II. Britain became a member in 1973.

SCIENCE AND DISCOVERY
DNA (deoxyribonucleic acid) was first defined as long ago as 1953, and the effects have been far-reaching. The key discovery was developed over the following years and today DNA fingerprinting has become an accepted part of life. Genetic diseases such as hemophilia and cystic fibrosis have been identified. Criminals are continually detected and brought to justice. Biological drugs have been developed. More controversially, drought and disease-resistant plants have been engineered - and Dolly the sheep has been produced.

Below: This genial pair of bakers with their toothy grins and their decorated, beflagged lorry formed part of Newbury's coronation procession in 1937. In fact this Hovis outfit has just been awarded first prize, winning them the princely sum of £10. Hovis used to be written in this rather idiosyncratic way with a dot above the 'o' to reflect the derivation of the name: it comes from the Latin 'hominis vis', meaning 'the strength of man'. Originally, when Richard Smith and Thomas Fitton founded the firm that was to become Hovis, they tried to market their flour under the rather less memorable brand name of Smith's Patent Germ Flour. Then in 1890, realising that a snappier name might help boost sales, they staged a national competition, offering a prize of £25 for the best suggestion; and having worked their way through the many, many entries which flooded in, they decided after much deliberation to award the prize to London student Herbert Grime who thought up Hovis. Posterity has proved that they made the right choice; sales improved, Hovis became a household name - and a rather nice postscript is that when Herbert died, the firm showed its appreciation by paying a pension to his widow as a tribute.

Right: To the uninitiated, this vehicle might look a little like a giant milk-float. In fact it is a Sentinel steam waggon, seen here at West Mills, taking in water from the river. Hovis ran a fleet of these vehicles, having acquired the first one - registration number YY 2387 - in 1931. They were used for carrying bulk wheat; throughout the 20s and in the early 30s, steam wagons were an attractive means of hauling heavy loads as they produced more power and were more economical to run than the petrol lorries of the day. The four-wheeler seen here was designed to carry seven tons; Sentinel also manufactured a six-wheeler to carry twelve ton loads, and a rigid eight-wheeler to carry fourteen tons. Later in the decade the heavy steam wagons were severely penalised by changes in the way vehicle taxation was levied. Great advances were being made by the manufacturers of diesel engines at around the same time, so many firms, including Hovis, switched to diesel lorries, and the steamer rapidly disappeared from our roads. Hovis itself remained in Newbury until 1957, having first moved there in 1921 when the company purchased Town Mill and West Mill from the Wallace family. When Hovis departed, Town Mill was occupied by Doltons until 1972, when it was demolished and replaced by flats.

Events of the 1950s

MELODY MAKERS
Few teenage girls could resist the blatant sex-appeal of 'Elvis the Pelvis', though their parents were scandalised at the moody Presley's provocatively gyrating hips. The singer took America and Britain by storm with such hits as 'Jailhouse Rock', 'All Shook Up' and 'Blue Suede Shoes'. The rhythms of Bill Haley and his Comets, Buddy Holly and Chuck Berry turned the 1950s into the Rock 'n' Roll years.

INVENTION AND TECHNOLOGY
Until the late 1950s you did not carry radios around with you. Radios were listened to at home, plugged into a mains socket in every average sitting room. Japan was in the forefront of electronic developments even then, and in 1957 the Japanese company Sony introduced the world's very first all-transistor radio - an item of new technology that was small enough to fit into your pocket. The major consumer product caught on fast - particularly with teenage listeners.

ROYAL WATCH
King George VI's health had been causing problems since 1948, when he developed thrombosis. In 1951 the King - always a heavy smoker - became ill again, and was eventually found to be suffering from lung cancer. His left lung was removed in September of 1951. In January 1952 he waved Princess Elizabeth and Prince Philip off on their tour of Africa; they were never to see him again. The King died in the early hours of 6th February 1952.

The very male crowd which has assembled to make its views known at this election meeting outside the Queen's Hotel reminds us that it is not so many generations since politics were an exclusively male province. Older readers may recall that Mrs Pankhurst's efforts were very recent history indeed when they were at school; in fact it was 1918 before women property-owners over the age of 30 were given the franchise, and not until 1928 that women gained the right to vote at 21, like the men. It is difficult

for today's emancipated young women to imagine life in the early 20th century, when they were expected to be essentially feminine and leave all the hard work and the thinking to the men - and apparently the champagne, too; we are told that when the Newbury Cinema opened in 1910, the gentlemen invited to the reception were offered champagne, and the ladies were offered 'fancy cakes'! The date of the election meeting shown here is not known, and we have to confess that we cannot name the MP who can be seen at the window, though if pressed we could hazard a tentative guess at General Clifton Brown or Frederic Mackarness . . . but we console ourselves with the thought that plenty of women living in Newbury at the time would not have known their MP's name, either!

You can't sneak up on the bright little chap on the left - he's spotted the photographer! And he'll probably get used to decimal currency a lot more quickly than many of his elders, too. We had been building up to D-day - Decimal day - for a long time. Decimal coins were phased in gradually, to give people chance to get used to them. The first batch of decimal coins was issued on April 23rd 1968, 50 pence pieces replaced ten shilling notes on October 14th 1969, and, as the large, clear notice in David Greggs' shop window tells us, decimal trading actually came into effect on February 16th 1971. Tanners, bobs and florins - alias two-bob bits - gradually disappeared from

DECIMAL TRADING
from TUESDAY 16th FEB: 1971

Prices marked & charged
in NEW PENCE

All Notes (£20, £10, £5, £1,)
AND
All Coins (50p, 10p, 2′, 5p, 1′, 6ᵈ, 2p, 1p, ½p.)
Accepted

To make it possible for us to give our
customers the exact change every time
THREEPENNY PIECES (3ᵈ) & OLD PENNIES (1ᵈ)
accepted ONLY in MULTIPLES of 6ᵈ

Change given in DECIMAL COINAGE (New pence)

DAVID GREIG

circulation. Many people hated decimalisation at first and some, including market traders, declared they would not use it. There was no denying that, in theory, decimal money was simpler than the old twelve pence to a shilling, twenty shillings to a pound system. In practice, prices marked in decimal money were meaningless at first, and the only way to decide whether an item was good value was by performing complicated mental arithmetic to translate decimal money back into good old shillings and pence! Many shops continued to display prices in both currencies for quite a time, while people got used to the new money and learned to 'think decimal'.

On the move

Before the construction of relief roads, heavy traffic had to pass through the centre of Newbury

The child in the pram by Boots probably breathed in a good lungful of diesel fumes on this day in 1960, as this heavy load made its way along Northbrook Street. With the A34 acting as the main trunk route connecting the Midlands, the traditional home of the heavy manufacturing industry, to the south of the country, it was inevitable that a lot of engineering products would pass through Newbury on their way to Southampton and other destinations in the south and south west. Before the construction of the relief roads, there was little option but to pass through the centre of Newbury. Half a decade after this photograph was taken, the route of the M4 had been decided upon, after much deliberation, and as the motorway network developed traffic planners were increasingly able to route their heavy loads along the roads designed to carry them, and so much misery was averted. Having said that, this particular load might have had to pass through Newbury anyway, as it looks suspiciously like a certain 90' by 14' fuel tank which is on record as having been delivered to Greenham air base.

This page and overleaf top: This particular vehicle appears to have been photographed twice - once in Cheap Street (where the angle of the front wheels suggests it is engaged in some delicate manoeuvring) with the clock showing just turned a quarter to eleven, and again in Northbrook Street, passing Marks & Spencer's clock at twenty to five. We sincerely hope that either one of the clocks was wrong, or two identical

loads passed through on different occasions - the idea of this monstrosity spending the whole day rumbling around the centre of Newbury makes the blood curdle. But sights such as this used to be all too common, since before the construction of the relief road

Events of the 1960s

WHAT'S ON?
Television comedy came into its own in the 1960s, and many of the shows that were favourites then went on to become classics. 'On the Buses', 'Steptoe and Son', 'Till Death Us Do Part' and 'The Army Game' kept audiences laughing, while the incredible talents of Morecambe and Wise, the wit of Des O'Connor - often the butt of the duo's jokes - and the antics of Benny Hill established them for ever in the nation's affections.

GETTING AROUND
The 2nd March 1969 was a landmark in the history of aviation. The Anglo-French supersonic airliner Concorde took off for the first time from Toulouse in France. Concorde, which can cruise at almost twice the speed of sound, was designed to fly from London to New York in an incredible three hours twenty minutes. The event took place just weeks after the Boeing 747, which can carry 500 passengers to Concorde's modest 100, made its first flight.

SPORTING CHANCE
Wembley Stadium saw scenes of jubilation when on 30th July 1966 England beat West Germany 4-2 in the World Cup. The match, played in a mixture of sunshine and showers, had been a nailbiting experience for players and spectators alike from the very beginning when Germany scored only thirteen minutes into the game. It was Geoff Hurst's two dramatic goals scored in extra time that secured the victory and lifted the cup for England - at last.

Northbrook Street was part of the main north-south route, bringing all the traffic travelling up and down the A34 straight through the centre of Newbury. This was bad enough in 1938, when there were almost two million cars in Britain; two decades later, when the number of private cars had risen by around 250 per cent and the volume of heavy loads travelling by road had increased tremendously as well, it had turned into a major headache. The problem was addressed in the 1950s, and a relief road scheme was devised to divert through traffic away from Speenhamland and Newbury centre. The east-west section was built first; Western Avenue and a new length of Bath Road opened in September 1961, followed by the construction of the Eastern Relief Road from St John's Road to Western Avenue in 1965, and in addition new plans for the town centre made better provision for off-street car parking. Problem solved! or so we all fondly hoped . . .

Left: This photograph could perhaps be construed as an object lesson in what Newbury has lost and why it

has lost it. 'Danger - Wide Load', proclaimed the truck, and the structures on the left-hand side were indeed in danger. Industry was expanding, the nation's lifestyle was changing, and the old town centre would soon come under pressure to keep pace, with new road layouts and new shopping facilities. The outside world could not be kept at bay much longer. None of the buildings on the west (left-hand) side of Cheap Street between the cameraman and the three-gabled house near the bend would survive for much more than a decade (assuming this picture to date from the late 50s - the sign for Carters Dyers on the right places it pre-1960, as by then Bollom had taken over from Carters). By the early 70s Fisher's and its neighbours had disappeared to allow traffic to sweep round in front of a new development of retail and office units, set back from the road. The new development is not without its critics, but equally the unfortunate shoppers pictured here cannot have vastly enjoyed waiting for this particular wide load to lumber past . . . followed by another . . . and then another . . .

Bottom: A stretch of Bartholomew Street featuring Whitehorn's, one time Newbury Model Bakeries, can be clearly seen in the background as we look across the car park which was created in Phase I of the Kennet development. Sainsbury's was an integral part of the first phase, as was the bus station which was built on the corner of Bartholomew Street and Market Street. The town clearly knew all the basic ingredients which it ultimately wanted to have in its new scheme of things - car parks, a bus station and new shops - but it was not until 1988, after building a multi-storey car park, knocking it down, putting a second new bus station where the car park had stood and turning the first bus station into more retail space, that it finally got everything in the right place. And then Sainsbury's moved . . . Meanwhile, however, we have an excellent overview of cars that Lord Sainsbury's customers favoured in 1972; and what is immediately striking is the absence of Japanese cars - the Far East had yet to make much of a mark on the motor industry - while a rough head-count confirms that the Mini was indeed, as we have always maintained, the most popular car of all.

Right: From a distance they might have resembled a flock of giant seagulls, but the party of hikers is now close enough to identify them as Armstrong-Whitworth Albemarles. This war-time photograph was taken at Hampstead Norrey's. The Albemarle - nicknamed Dumbo - was originally designed as a medium bomber and reconnaissance plane. However, between 1939 when the prototype was

created and late 1941 when production began, the design was modified, and of the 602 Albemarles which were built, the majority were adapted to special transport and glider-tug duties. The latter role is probably the one with which most people associated them, and they are best remembered for their part in landing our troops behind the enemy lines in the D-Day landing, dropping parachute troops and towing Horsa gliders made by Airspeed of Portmouth, with Elliotts' factory in Newbury involved in their production. In addition to the Normandy invasion in 1944, Albemarles were also used on a number of other occasions including the invasion of Sicily in July 1943 - their first use on operations - and the Arnhem landing in September 1944.

What a parade!

Rain will not stop this parade; the crowd's umbrellas are up, but the troops do not bat an eyelid. The YMCA sign on the Plaza tells us that we are looking at a wartime scene. Between 1935 and 1945 the Plaza served as the YMCA canteen, and many a young GI, newly flown in from across the Atlantic, must have been relieved to find a friendly face and good British cup of tea waiting there to welcome him to Newbury. Built in 1925 on the site of the old King's Arms, versatility was all part of the Plaza's raison d'etre. It was planned by James Tufnail, Newbury's mercurial newsagent, as a shopping arcade and multi-purpose entertainment venue. Many plays,

films and other events were staged there, as well as regular dances and, from time to time, roller-skating, as it had a sprung floor. Stories about its founder are rife - for instance, it is reported that after resigning from the town council he sent each councillor a mousetrap by way of insult, and that during the construction of the Plaza he laid a stone bearing the inscription: 'This stone was laid by James Tufnail. A man who could never suitably describe the Robbery Corporation without using bad language.' Having resided in Newbury for 43 years and contributed a certain piquancy to town life, this dynamic and outspoken figure died in 1930.

Market Place has been the scene of innumerable parades and marchpasts, both during the war and afterwards; wartime parades were an effective way of keeping morale up and making sure that the war effort did not lose impetus. This photograph shows a Battle of Britain marchpast, though we have been unable to ascertain the exact date. The banner across the front of the Corn Exchange bears the message: Be sure to be here next week - Take care not risks, and while we agree wholeheartedly with the sentiment, we must confess to finding its context somewhat enigmatic; is it a reference to wartime security? or to a road safety or even an inoculation

Events of the 1960s

HOT OFF THE PRESS
Barbed wire, concrete blocks and a wide no-man's-land divided East from West when a reinforced wall was built right across the city of Berlin in 1961. Many East Germans escaped to the West at the eleventh hour, taking with them only the possessions they could carry. The Berlin Wall divided the city - and hundreds of family members and friends - for 28 years until the collapse of Communist rule across Eastern Europe. Who can ever forget those scenes in 1989, when ordinary people themselves began to physically tear down the hated wall?

THE WORLD AT LARGE
'One giant leap for mankind' was taken on 20th July 1969, when Neil Armstrong made history as the first man to set foot on the moon. During the mission he and fellow-astronaut 'Buzz' Aldrin collected rock and soil samples, conducted scientific experiments - and had a lot of fun jumping around in the one-sixth gravity. Twenty-one hours and thirty-seven minutes after their landing they took off again in their lunar module 'Eagle' to rejoin Apollo II which was orbiting above them, proudly leaving the American flag on the Moon's surface.

ROYAL WATCH
Princess Margaret's announcement in 1960 that she was to wed photographer Antony Armstrong-Jones (later Lord Snowdon) brought sighs of relief from her immediate family. Just five years earlier the people of Britain had sympathised as the princess bowed to public and private pressure, ending her relationship with Peter Townsend, Prince Philip's former equerry. The Church (and the Queen, as its Head) frowned on the liaison as Townsend was divorced. Her marriage to Lord Snowdon itself ended in 1978.

campaign staged in later years? The presence of so many men on this photograph suggest that this particular marchpast took place after the war. September 15th was designated Battle of Britain day, and although perhaps it is celebrated to lesser extent these days than formerly, still each year a variety of events are staged to commemorate our success in repelling Germany's airborne attack.

Right: The Scots and Irish Guards made a fine sight as they marched through Newbury on 15th September 1957 - the day of the Agricultural Show, held at Elcot. Though its origins do not go as far back as those of the market and the fair, the Agricultural Show has established itself as one of Newbury's traditions. It is thought that a Show was in existence by 1840; the Newbury Agricultural Society was formed in 1909 and put on its first Newbury Show on 9th November of that year at Enborne Gate Farm. The Show has had a number venues. Elcot Park was its regular home between 1936 and 1963, with a break during the war, and since then it has been held at, Siege, Henwick Court and Priors Court. The 1957 Show's success can be gauged by its vital statistics: 15,000 people passed through the gates at Elcot Park - 4,000 more than the previous year - and there were a record number of entries which included 481 cattle, nearly 200 pigs and 24 pens of sheep. Other attractions included a parade by the Coldstream Guards. Many people commented on how well-organised the Show was, and it was pronounced the best one-day event of its kind anywhere in the country.

Below: There was widespread agreement that Newbury's Jubilee decorations in 1935 were the best of any town outside London. Here we can see the bunting out across Northbrook Street and the Union Jacks fluttering outside the shops as the parade marches past. There was plenty going on 9th May 1935: as well as street parties and carnival parades, Newbury's great civic event was the opening of the new sports pavilion, bowling green and tennis courts in Victoria Park, the impressive outcome of a scheme to provide local employment. And for the children - well, there were free shows at the cinemas, with around 2,000 kids squeezing in to the Regal and the Carlton to enjoy such treats as Mickey Mouse cartoons and Frank Titterton singing The King's Song, there were free teas laid on in all the public halls, and there was a free Jubilee beaker for every child, presented by the Mayor, Councillor C W Burns, in person. How many readers still have their Jubilee beakers, we wonder? Then in the evening a great bonfire was lit on Sidown Hill on Highclere Park estate; this bonfire was one in a chain of beacons which spread right across the country as the whole nation joined together in celebrating the Silver Jubilee of their beloved monarch, King George V.

Edinburgh's Royal Regiment (inevitably acquiring a new nickname from the abbreviation 1DERR - Wonder). Thirty-five years later further change came about in the form of an amalgamation with the Gloucestershire Regiment, creating the regiment known since 1994 as the Royal Gloucestershire Berkshire and Wiltshire Regiment.

Top: The young man is concentrating hard on holding his placard high, and the women - presumably auxiliary nurses - have determined expressions and a very purposeful air about them; but quite what that purpose was, we can at this stage only guess at. However, if the exact occasion is not recorded, we can at least identify the location: they are marching along Northbrook Street,

Above: Eyes right! The Royal Berkshire Regiment - affectionately known as The Biscuit Boys, the Farmers' Boys, The Brave Boys of Berkshire or alternatively The China Dragons (after the dragon on its cap badge) - marches past the official party on the dais on Wednesday, July 23rd 1947, along a Northbrook Street thronged with crowds who have turned out to see their local military heroes. Honoured on that date by the presentation of the Freedom of Newbury, this great regiment retained the Freedom even when reorganisation brought its existence as a separate entity to an end. In 1959 the Royal Berkshire Regiment merged with the Wiltshire Regiment to form the Duke of

past Baylis & Co, the grocers, and Dexter Robinson the draper. Clothes suggest the inter-war period, and to those of us who today think of the squash as a game invented to allow high-powered young business executives and stressed-out middle management to burn off their pent-up aggression and frustration, the lettering advertising the existence of squash courts might come as rather a surprise - executive stress is not a syndrome one associates with the 1930s. But certainly by 1937 there was a squash club at 6 Pembroke Road. Later on, during the latter years of the war, the squash club was adapted to act as a hostel and canteen run by the Red Cross for US servicemen.

Market Place has resounded to the music of military bands and the sound of marching feet on countless occasions over the years. There is something irresistible about the pomp and pageantry of a parade: no matter how many marching bands you've seen before, and no matter how busy you are, it is hard to resist the temptation to stop what you're doing and watch. On this occasion dense crowds have gathered around Market Place, while other spectators are enjoying a grandstand view from the upper storey windows. The

reason for particular civic ceremony has been lost in the mists of time, unless any readers are able to shed any light. However, Polyfotos - as advertised above Hickman & Metcalf - certainly bring back memories. They were popular in the 50s, and provided many tiny, black and white photographs to a page, which could then be snipped of and sent to aunts, uncles and second cousins twice removed to help them keep track of new babies and growing children - ideal for those with large, far-flung families.

The Royal Berkshire Regiment was granted the Freedom of the town of Newbury in July 1947

Wednesday July 23rd 1947 was a great day for the Royal Berkshire Regiment. On that date the Regiment was granted the Freedom of the town of Newbury, to record, in the words of the Mayor, Mr A V Bradshaw, 'the abiding pride in the record and achievement of the Regiment.' Crowds had gathered to watch the Freedom ceremony, which took place in Market Place, and the Mayor's words 'abiding pride' must surely have summed up everyone's feelings as they watched the lines of smart, brave, upright soldiers - particularly those who had relatives or friends in the ranks. The honour guard, which was inspected by the Mayor and General Sir Miles Dempsey, Colonel of the Regiment, included L/Cpl Brian Barlow and L/Cpl Ted Warne, both of Newbury. The climax of the proceedings was the presentation by the Mayor of the Scroll conferring the Freedom of Newbury, together with a silver bugle which had been raised by subscription from the people of the town.

Above: This Mayor's Sunday photograph shows Councillor Reginald John Brighton Croft Huckle, the newly-elected Mayor of Newbury, in procession to the Methodist Church on Northbrook Street on 30th May 1954. Mr Huckle had played an active role since coming to Newbury in 1937, taking on a wide range of committee duties which included responsibility for the improvements to Victoria Park and for Newbury's Coronation decorations. Newbury's mayor's chain is a particularly fine one, and has an interesting history. The chain itself dates back to 1884, but the beautiful pendant seen here is newer. Former Mayor Jack Hole (who also revived an old tradition by contributing a new link to the chain) was instrumental in the creation of the crest, which is composed of the ear of corn to represent agriculture in the town, the teasel as a symbol of the textile industry, a wavy line to denote the river, and a castle - Donnington - in the background, while the ornamentation surrounding it signifies Borough status and the greater responsibilities which rested upon the council prior to the reorganisation which transferred many of its duties to West Berkshire County Council.

Above right: If company mission statements had been in vogue in 1930, then the Forum, seen here in the early 60s, would no doubt have set as its objective 'to be the best cinema in Newbury'. It opened on 6th November 1930, with seating for over a thousand, including a number of seats equipped with earphones for the deaf, and declared its intention 'to take account of local tastes in choosing features' - and it started off well, showing Trouble Brewing with George Formby in the first week. But inevitably it began to struggle when

television and then video arrived. Taken over by the ABC by the time of this photograph, it was refurbished in August 1972 and tried to make a go of it as a smaller 480-seat cinema with a bingo hall downstairs. Towards the end of the 80s the bingo hall closed and the Cannon chain took the cinema over, but it was becoming clear that its days were numbered. Having survived for almost 68 years, and outlasted all Newbury's other cinemas, on Sunday 1st November 1998 it finally closed its doors. The last film shown was Small Soldiers, which brings us neatly back to our photograph - except that these soldiers aren't small; they are the ATC 211 Newbury Squadron, standing straight and tall. The Newbury Air Transport Corps squadron was formed in February 1941, and local youngsters were delighted to have the opportunity of enrolling in such a glamorous outfit.

Pages 81-84: Newbury's American connection began with the arrival of US troops when America joined the Allies in the second world war in 1942. The arrival of so many unfamiliar uniforms and unfamiliar voices created quite a stir, but soon the polite, friendly young men were accepted by the town. They in their turn appreciated Newbury's hospitality; typical of the young servicemen's kindness and generosity were the little treats they planned for children in hospital. By the time they departed at the end of the war, not only had they won our respect and gratitude for the part they played in winning the war - many of the Americans who were landed in Normandy as part of the D Day

Events of the 1960s

MELODY MAKERS
The 1960s: those were the days when the talented blues guitarist Jimi Hendrix shot to rock stardom, a youthful Cliff Richard charmed the nation with his 'Congratulations' and Sandie Shaw won the Eurovision Song Contest for Britain with 'Puppet on a String'. It was the combined musical talents of a group of outrageous working-class Liverpool lads, however, who formed the Beatles and took the world by storm with music that ranged from the experimental to ballads such as 'Yesterday'.

INVENTION AND TECHNOLOGY
A major step forward was made in 1960 when the laser was invented. An acronym for Light Amplification by Stimulated Emission of Radiation, the device produces a narrow beam of light that can travel for vast distances and is focused to give enormous power. Laser beams, as well as being able to carry far more information than radio waves, can also be used for surgery, cutting, drilling, welding and scores of other operations.

SCIENCE AND DISCOVERY
When the drug Thalidomide was first developed during the 1950s it was hailed as a wonder drug which would ease the distressing symptoms of pregnancy sickness. By the early 1960s the drug's terrible side effects were being discovered, when more than 3000 babies had been born with severe birth defects. Malformed limbs, defective eyes and faulty intestines were the heart-rending legacy left by Thalidomide.

invasion of Europe were based at Greenham - but a considerable number had also won the hearts of Newbury girls. When they left, accompanied in some cases by their brides, the town

seemed suddenly quiet. Our own men came back from the war and housing became a problem, so Greenham Common was used by Newbury Rural

District Council to provide temporary accommodation in Nissen huts while a major house-building programme was put into effect; by July 1948, 136

new dwellings had been constructed. Then in 1951 the American air force was back in residence at Greenham. An on-going programme of development work began. In November 1952 the main road from Newbury to Basingstoke was closed to permit the airfield to be extended, and a new road was opened, running from Newtown along the southern edge of the common. By 1953 the USAF 303rd Bomber Wing was in occupation, equipped with six-engined B47 Stratojets able to carry nuclear bombs, and they

It was agreed that America should withdraw from British air bases and they vacated Greenham on 30th June 1964

remained at Greenham for more than a decade while high-level political debate went on between the British and American authorities about the future of the nuclear programme; and at a local level irate individuals made complaints from time to time about aircraft noise. Eventually it was agreed that America should withdraw from British air bases, and they vacated Greenham on 30th June 1964. These photographs were taken during their farewell parade through Newbury.

Shopping spree

Marks & Spencer Ltd's brand new store seems to be getting a final spit and polish prior to opening its doors to the public on May 1st, 1935. Crowds of people turned up to the grand opening, eager to inspect the range of goods on offer - and the opening of the store was good news for those lucky enough to have found jobs there, too, as Marks & Spencer were offering higher wages than most other local shops. The Marks & Spencer chain was founded by Michael Marks and Tom Spencer in 1894, who opened their first shops under the name of Penny Bazaar. By 1915 Messrs Marks and Spencer had opened 140 Penny Bazaars throughout the country - not a bad rate of return from an investment of £300, representing a half-share in the enterprise! The name Marks & Spencer first appeared above a store up in Darlington in 1922. Marks & Sparks' Newbury store was built on the site of the old Jack of Newbury Hotel, which had had to be demolished when it was discovered that death watch beetle had wreaked havoc with the roof. Jack o' Newbury himself, 'the most considerable clothier England ever beheld', used to occupy this spot, and no doubt he would have been very interested to see how the clothing retail trade has developed in the last 500 years . . .

Below: Mr and Mrs Hazell, together with Rose Hazell (on the left) and assistant Mr E Mason, have stepped outside for a moment to pose for the photographer outside their hardware stores at number 11, London Road. The store, which was run by the family until the late 1950s, is seen here in 1938, crammed full of household items that will bring back memories of the days before plastic. Hanging up are oval galvanised baths (in which babies were bathed, on the hearthrug in front of a blazing fire), a cane laundry basket (remember the comfortable creaking noise they used to make when they were carried downstairs, piled high with the weekly wash?) and a wash board - wash boards, of course, were to take on a whole new function in life when Lonnie Donegan used them to create the skiffle sound that swept the nation in the 50s. Then there are mats, galvanised buckets and wood-and-bristle broom heads of all different sizes. A large sign advertises gold paint, but we were not yet a nation of DIY-ers; painting and decorating was generally left to the professionals until after the second world war, and it was not until 1953 that Dulux came onto the retail market.

Just look at what you got for your money in the 50s - for one-and-fourpence (7p in today's currency) you could have a pound of tomatoes or 'special bananas', while choice peaches would set you back seven bob (35p). This well-stocked fruit shop on London Road is a clear indication that that the wartime ration books and the tiresome going-without-and-making-do regime are all well and truly over at last - no more grey bread with the curious little black bits in it, no more powdered eggs, and no more optimistically relying on those highly imaginative Ministry of Food recipes week

after week to miraculously transform the same bland ingredients into a tempting meal; some recipes turned out surprisingly well, but some didn't. During the war years bananas disappeared from our shops so completely that by the time they came back we had a generation of toddlers who had never eaten a banana in their lives. It was brought home to us just how long the banana had been absent from these shores when we saw that our little ones were quite at a loss as to how to eat them, and had to be initiated into the art of skinning a banana!

At work

A far cry from today's unisex salons, the advertisements for cigarettes and tobacco, the Rugby fixtures list and the cabinet full of hair oils and suchlike firmly proclaim this to be a man's world. In the 1950s men did not have their hair highlighted or permed - what, sit there under a hairdryer like a woman? A short back and sides was the order of the day, and all a chap had to decide was, which side to have his parting. The only exception to the rule was the occasional teddy-boy quiff or DA. Not for another decade would the Beatles encourage widespread insurrection among boys, and turn the length of one's hair into a lifestyle issue; until then, as soon as a boy's hair reached his ears or touched his collar, he would be despatched to the barber's with his tanner (6d) for a haircut. We believe this particular photograph to have been taken inside Bradshaw's at 1, Bartholomew Road, though any readers who have reason to think otherwise will no doubt let us know.

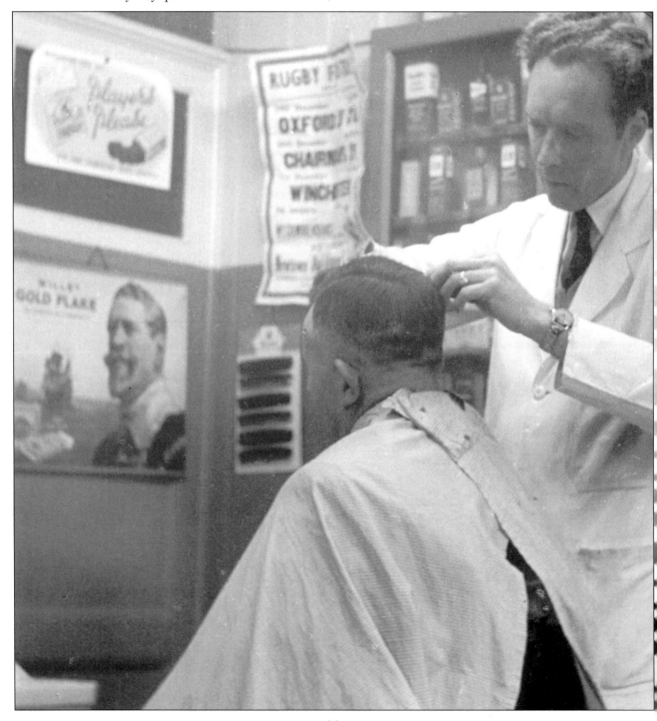

many companies who started out in the excavating and earth moving industries has become heavily involved in waste management; environmental awareness is one sphere where as a nation we seem to have made great progress in recent years, and being green has taken on a completely different meaning!

Top: A sight which the majority of readers will have seen many, many times at the end of a day's trading on the market. Newbury has remained very much a market town at heart. It was officially granted a Market Charter towards the end of the 16th century, although certainly the market began long before that, possibly even as early as the 12th century. Over the years we have had a rich collection of colourful characters manning the stalls, and it is these unfailingly cheerful personalities, as much as the bargains that are to be had - everything from cheap, good quality fruit and vegetables and household utensils to cut-price clothes and fancy goods - that help create the special market atmosphere and make a trip round the stalls such a tonic. Stories and jokes are swapped amidst all the good-natured hustle and bustle, shopping bags begin to bulge with bargains too good to miss, and as five o'clock approaches Market Place rings with the cries of stallholders cajoling shoppers into buying up the last of their stock. But readers will no doubt all have their own favourite market memories . . .

Above: Hills' fleet of red lorries, seen here at the company's plant on Hambridge Road, have long been a familiar sight around Newbury. Gravel extraction began at Hambridge Road around the late 30s; by 1969, when this photograph was taken, excavation was still going on in the neighbourhood though not at this particular site. Mixconcrete Ltd, whose plant can be seen on the right, were in fact a separate company, and were supplied with aggregate by Hills Limited. Hills carried on digging in the area right up until the late 80s, after which their site at Hambridge Road was filled in and sold, and an industrial estate was built on the land. Hills, now the Hills Group, is still active in the area, and like

Livestock sales were a part of Newbury life for centuries

Many Newbury people still regret the loss of the Cattle Market. Livestock sales were part of Newbury life for centuries; at one time farmers from the surrounding area used to buy and sell cattle in Market Place, and then it became the practice for auctions to be conducted in the yards of certain inns, made available for the day. Later Market Street was used, where in 1873 a new Cattle Market was opened by the Earl of Carnarvon. This market was extended in 1918, resulting in the familiar Cattle Market seen on this picture. Over the years the number of beasts sold decreased, but on Mondays and Thursdays, when the streets were full of the sounds and smells of livestock on their way to market, there was a special atmosphere which contrasted with the increasingly urbanised town centre. Observers, particularly young-sters, loved to mingle with the crowd of farmers, soaking up the atmosphere and listening to the auctioneer's patter. However, by the late 60s there were new trends in farming: cereal growing was becoming more important, and there was an increasing tendency throughout the country for livestock sales to be concen-trated in fewer, larger centres. So in 1968, Newbury's Cattle Market was closed.

It's just a matter of course

Aglance through Newbury College's prospectus for the last year of the millennium reveals classes in everything from Feng Shui to Philosophy, Motorcycle Maintenance to Bridge, and Morse Code to Tap Dancing - in addition to a wide variety of courses leading to professional trade and business qualifications. Further education - whether as a leisure activity, for career advancement or in order to keep abreast of new technology - has become an accepted part of contemporary life. This was not always the case, however, and the fact that these days we can take further education for granted is due in no small part to the efforts of institutions such as Newbury College, which have over many years devoted themselves to building up the facilities and the expertise to bring us such an excellent provision.

Newbury College has been in existence for over 50 years, although not always under that name. Known first as the Newbury Institute of Further Education, it then became the South Berkshire College of Further Education, and was re-christened Newbury College in 1975. The Institute of Further Education was established in 1948, and took over the role of providing practical and vocational education for the people of Newbury - a role which had been carried out in the early part of the 20th century by the Technical Institute. Housed in premises at 60 Northbrook Street and financed by Berkshire County Council, the Institute had run evening classes in subjects such as building construction, mechanical engineering, shorthand and book-keeping. Courses were strictly vocational; the Institute liaised with local employers to ensure that its provision met the needs of industry and commerce. The 1929-30 Prospectus specified that 'The classes are intended for those whose ordinary occupation or employment occupies the greater part of their time and must not be attended by children who are at school', and records show

that established local firms such as Plenty's, Camp Hopson and Hoskings & Pond regularly sent their apprentices to the Technical Institute.

The Technical Institute became part of the Newbury Institute of Further Education in 1948. Radical reform of the educational system was taking place all over the country around this time; Berkshire County Council set up Institutes of Further Education in Maidenhead, Newbury and Windsor, which were 'to be responsible primarily for the development of further education, both technical and adult, in day and evening activities'. Again, great emphasis was attached to making provision for apprentices, and employers were now encouraged to release them to attend daytime classes.

It was a fortunate coincidence that, just at the time when plans for the new Institute were being made, Ormonde House was standing empty. This fine Victorian country

Below: *Ladies' keep fit classes.*
Bottom: *Dressmaking classes.*

all the teaching but the Principal as well. Albert Owthwaite, the first Principal or Superintendent as he was initially known, occupied the top floor and part of the first floor - for which 18/- a week was deducted from his annual salary of between £700 and £850. During the Autumn term, 1948, a total of 1,000 students enrolled for the 50 classes on offer. The following term additional classes were arranged for motor vehicle apprentices and apprentice electricians, particularly those working for the Southern Electricity Board. In all, 158 students were able to take advantage of the innovative day release option during the course of the first year. At the same time the new Institute's 71 evening classes were attended by a further 1,350 students - more than three times the number of students who had enrolled at the Technical Institute the previous year.

house at 38 Oxford Road had remained a private residence until the second world war. Its occupants had included racehorse trainer John Porter, who had named it after his great racehorse Ormonde. During the war years Ormonde House had provided a temporary home for St Gabriel's School, and when they moved to Sandleford at the end of the war, 38 Oxford Road was bought by Berkshire County Council. It is still at the centre of the College today, although the site has changed almost beyond recognition, having spread to almost twice the size through the acquisition of land to the south, 36 Oxford Road (now demolished) to the south-west, and a large plot of land formerly occupied by Marlborough House to the north. This expansion has been a gradual process, reflecting the growth of the College.

When the Newbury Institute opened in 1948, however, Ormonde House was large enough to accommodate not only

Successive years brought increased student numbers, and by 1951 classroom accommodation was at a premium. Dressmaking and embroidery took over the conservatory, while other classes including technical drawing, brickwork and plumbing spilled out into the outbuildings - a couple of wooden sheds, a greenhouse, a garage and even, for some

Above left: The main entrance in the 1950s.
Top: Ballroom dancing in 1952.
Right: A 1959 drama class.

lucky students, a chicken shed! The building apprentices put up a Nissen hut and used it for their workshop. Still there was not enough space, and classes spread into part of the old Technical Institute in Northbrook Street and a miscellany of schools and other buildings. Clearly a crisis was developing; however, 1951 brought further reorganisation, and among the plans and proposals agreed between the Government and Berkshire County Council was the premises of new, purpose-built accommodation.

Other organisational changes resulted in Newbury Institute becoming the headquarters of South Berkshire College, which now had responsibility for further education provision in the south-western part of the county. Albert Owthwaite remained as Principal; his staff now numbered 10 full-time lecturers and 61 part-time assistants, as compared to two full-time lecturers and a collection of part-time instructors paid by the hour in 1948-49. The list of courses had also grown tremendously, and one significant development was the provision of full-time courses for school-leavers, beginning with a commercial course and a pre-apprenticeship course in building and engineering and going on to include full-time dressmaking and domestic science, secretarial and General Certificate of Education courses. During the 1950s the student population included significant contingents of trainees from local employers - electricians from the SEB, engineers from Plenty's, Newbury Diesel Company, Opperman Gears, the Colthrop board mills; motor vehicle technicians from Marchants, Martin & Chillingworth, Murray & Whittakers and others, and builders, of whom many were engaged on the construction of the Valley Road Estate, as well as a small but growing number of full-time students - 26 in 1951-52, rising to 55 by 1956-7. The part-time and full-time modes of study were subsequently complemented by a third option when block release was introduced in 1966, allowing craft apprentices to attend the College for one week in every three. And from 1952 onwards the Atomic

Energy establishments at Harwell and Aldermaston also began sending their staff to the South Berkshire College; over the next 30 years or so these two establishments were the source of literally hundreds of students, and this was a very significant factor in the consolidation and growth of the College in the 60s.

Berkshire County Council recognised that there was an urgent need to improve the College's accommodation to enable it to meet the demands of its students, and the arrival of the two Atomic Energy establishments on its doorstep was perceived as adding a degree of urgency to the situation. As an interim measure, two prefabs - one of which is still part of the College today - were installed and officially opened on the Open Day in the summer of 1953. The annual timetabling exercise continued to rely heavily on the greenhouse and other outbuildings - and from the late 50s featured the conservatory in its new role as a chemistry laboratory! Help was at hand, however. The first instalment of the permanent building programme comprised specialist workshops and laboratories for building, engineering and science courses, and was completed in 1956 - the year in which Eric Lansley took over as Principal from Albert Owthwaite. By 1960 the second instalment was also complete, providing specialist

Right: *The 1962 Pre-apprenticeship class.*
Below: *Country dancing in Coronation Hall in the 50s.*

training accommodation, a Hall, a refectory and a library. The addition of two more permanent buildings during the 1960s meant that the College no longer had to rely on garden sheds and empty rooms in the town centre for its teaching accommodation.

The College was guided through the 60s by Eric Lansley, and in 1970 he was succeeded by Roy Pocock, whose long and productive association with the institution had begun when he joined the Newbury Institute as its third full-time lecturer. He retired in 1979, having made a tremendous contribution to the development of further education in south-west Berkshire. Eric Memmott then became Principal of Newbury College, as it had become known; extensive development of the site continued throughout this period, and a number of neighbouring buildings including number 36 Oxford Road and Marlborough House were demolished to create more space for buildings and car parks. The final brick building was installed in the mid 80s, and this houses the Donnington Room training restaurant and the College Library.

In 1993 the present Principal, Gordon Bull, took up post, and the following year Berkshire County Council relinquished control of the establishment and Newbury College was incorporated as an independent institution. Thus it is now better placed than ever to fulfil its mission of providing lifelong education and training opportunities for the community, with the College's very flexible curriculum currently attracting around 20,000 students a year, of whom more than a third are full-time. Its high standards of excellence have repeatedly won official recognition; Newbury College regularly scores highly in the annual appraisal exercise carried out by the Further Education Funding Council, and other recent achievements include winning two huge awards worth £450,000 each to support high technology initiatives in West Berkshire.

Newbury College has taken on an increasingly important role in the community over the last 50 years. It has grown from a small institution staffed by a couple of full-time lecturers and offering a handful of part-time courses for local apprentices into a major provider of high-quality further education. It has overcome the challenges of delivering an increasing range of courses in inadequate accommodation. As the next millennium approaches it is looking forward to moving to new state-of-the-art premises on a 40-acre site off Monks Lane, near the Rugby Club. The new premises, designed especially for Newbury College and expected to be ready early in 2001, will provide exciting prospects for this dynamic College to enhance its already excellent education provision. The people of Newbury can look forward to an even wider choice of learning opportunities in the years to come.

Many thanks to Malcolm Phillips for his input into this piece

Above left: *A 1970s engineering class.* ***Top:*** *The workshops and laboratories at the rear of Ormonde House.* ***Right:*** *Gordon Bull - Chief Executive and Principal.* ***Below:*** *An artist's impression of how the new College will look.*

Let them eat cake...and bread as well!

Up with the dawn, deliveries till late...it had been a long day for baker Henry Thomas Hussey, and he was looking forward to a pint or three at the George & Horn. Leaving his horse and delivery cart outside, he joined his pals for a well-deserved evening of relaxation in the pub. A few hours later, his family heard the familiar sound of wheels on the cobbles as the cart pulled into the yard and they knew that Bess had done it again. Eager for her supper, the faithful old horse - with Henry fast asleep in the cart - had once more made a beeline for home.

There was little time for relaxation in a busy baker's life. This after all was a family business after the old tradition, and the entire Hussey family was involved in building on the successful business founded by Henry's father James in the 1870s. Every member of the workforce had to be Jack of all trades (and master of all), with a finger in every pie, so to speak.... In those days it was muscle power alone that hoisted the heavy hessian sacks of flour and carried wooden buckets of water from the well - a far cry from today's lifts, ramps and computerised systems! The first world war saw women employed in all areas of the business, including those that had up to that time been seen as 'jobs for the boys'. It was a tradition that was to remain a part of wartime Britain, seen again during the second world war when men were called into military service. War and its aftermath brought its own difficulties and challenges, and even after peace was declared in 1945 Hussey's were not out of the woods. A year after the end of the war, bread went on ration for the first time. The numerous setbacks, however, had the effect of making every member of staff work together towards a common goal. And through it all they established the principle that has remained an integral part of the bakery to the present day: excellent quality coupled with exceptional service to the customer. To this end, Hussey's continue to ensure their success by investing in people.

Today the bakery is busier than ever before, with four retail outlets which are in demand locally as breakfast and lunchtime takeaways, and more than 1,500 deliveries made

Above: *The Hussey family.*
Below: *The original house and bakery.*

members toiled in days gone by have given way to up-to-date oil fired ovens. Provers, automated packing machines, bread slicers, cooling and refrigeration equipment, even metal detectors, have been installed, and bakers work around the clock to produce the freshest possible goods using the finest ingredients. A state of the art computerised office system guarantees the smooth running of the bakery, and orders are speedily and efficiently processed. Long before most people's alarm clocks go off, Hussey's packers are already hard at work assembling orders and loading the vans for despatch and rapid delivery.

on Hussey's own vehicles every day to the retail and catering trade. Two supermarket groups sell a wide range of Hussey's products in a number of different outlets. In addition a large range of Hussey's innovative and specialist products are blast frozen and packed into boxes and sold through frozen food distributors to pubs, hotels, canteens and restaurants. An incredible range of more than 250 breads, rolls and pastries are produced daily to order, with no minimum delivery quantity.

Michael Hussey, great-grandson of James Hussey, chairs the bakery today, and he combines modern production methods with family recipes handed down over the company's long history. Still based in Ashford Hill near the M4, the modern, purpose-built bakery bears no resemblance to the premises of old. Electric mixers and processing equipment have replaced the wooden dough troughs and knives used by his grandfather and great-grandfather, and the old fashioned wood fired bread oven where family

Under the able leadership of Graham Last (Managing Director), a team of experts has been built up over the years, with Malcolm Squires (Accountant), Andy Rogers (Bakery Manager), Flemming Westphalen (QA/Technical Manager), Jon Hotchkiss (Distribution Manager), David Trickey responsible for sales and Barbara Godby for administration. The management team, coupled with a wealth of staff experience, many with a substantial number of years' service, aim to make the customers' needs the prior concern of the business.

And what of the future? Well, 1999 saw the company for the first time exhibiting at the International Food Exhibition held at Earls Court which opened many new and exciting doors and subsequently saw the company attend a similar event in Spain. Overall there is a desire to continue to build on their past achievements in a world dominated by giant companies and to continue offering secure employment, quality products and an excellent service to every customer.

Above left: *Part of the 1980s fleet.*
Top: *An aerial view of the premises today.*

Valuing both clients and their property

In 1759 a craftsman named Thomas Davis came to Newbury from Abingdon. By trade a brazier, upholsterer and cabinet maker, he set up in business at 22 Market Place. He also offered his services as 'appraiser', which would have involved valuing furniture and household effects. He took additional premises on Northbrook Street, and it is thought that these became his offices while the house on Market Place was the family home and craft workshop. In 1770 Thomas Davis advertised two farms to let on the Sydmonton estate; this marked the beginning of his involvement in agricultural work, and he went on to conduct frequent sales of livestock and machinery as well as of household furniture. Soon the agricultural community began to come to him for advice on estate management; he then started to handle the sale of farms themselves, which in turn led to the sale of private houses.

The business remained in the family for three generations after Thomas' death in 1794, passing first to his son William until his death in 1836, and subsequently to William's son Alexander, a man of outstanding ability whose straightforward approach to business was appreciated by all who had dealings with him. Alexander Davis ran the firm from 1836 until his retirement in 1884, when the business was carried on by Harry Few, who had become a partner three years earlier. Harry subsequently amalgamated with another Auctioneer, Thomas Dreweatt, who had set up in business some time previously; the partnership lasted for four years, and Thomas Dreweatt then became sole partner following Mr Few's retirement in 1888. Ten years later Arthur Watson became a joint partner, and in 1919 the firm took on the title of Dreweatt, Watson & Barton by which it was known for many decades when Harold Barton, who had joined the firm in 1910, became a third partner.

Meanwhile another successful family auctioneers' business had grown up in Newbury. Arthur Webb Neate lived at Anville Farm, Hungerford after completing his articles; he had an office at 108 High Street, and records show that he conducted an auction of live and dead farm stock at Oxenwood Farm in September 1876. He opened an office at Albion House, Oxford Road, Newbury during the 1880s, and the business continued as a family firm; Arthur's two younger sons Frank and Stephen were taken into partnership after the first world war and the firm was renamed A W Neate & Sons. They, like their rival Dreweatt, Watson & Barton, dealt mainly with agricultural work. In the late 1920s they started an estate agency, and also had a furniture saleroom at the rear of the Cheap Street Office; this site subsequently became the Baptist Church. A spirit of healthy competition developed between the two firms. Dreweatt, Watson & Barton notched up one notable victory, however - they managed to become the first firm in the whole of Newbury to be installed with the telephone, enjoying

Above left: Thomas Davis. **Below:** *The firm's premises at 22 Market Place in the 1930s.*

integrity, personal attention and quality of service, it is the firm's belief that an understanding of people's needs is of paramount importance in meeting the challenges of contemporary life, since dealing with property means dealing with the people who own, occupy, use, buy or sell that property. The firm places great emphasis on professional development, team-work and individual responsibility, and this is reflected in its Investor in People status. For approaching 250 years the people of Newbury have relied on the advice of Dreweatt Neate; and through dealing with the changes which have taken place in this period the firm has built up an unrivalled understanding of the region's needs. This, combined with its modern outlook and its friendly attitude, will stand it in excellent stead in the future.

for many, many years the ultimate in distinctive phone numbers - Newbury 1. By 1959, the year in which Dreweatt, Watson & Barton celebrated its bi-centenary, the Barton family was still very active in the firm. A W Neate & Sons, meanwhile, had departed from tradition in 1950 by taking its first non-family member, John Pallett, into the business.

The friendly rivalry between Dreweatt, Watson & Barton and A W Neate & Sons continued for over a century in all, but finally drew to its logical conclusion in 1988 when, in an economic climate increasingly dominated by large conglomerates, the two merged to form Dreweatt Neate. The current Managing Partner, Martin Lowry, had joined the firm through a merger between Neates and Pink Donger & Lowry (founded 1849) some three years previously.

Dreweatt Neate is today a successful Chartered Surveyors and Fine Art Auctioneers with offices throughout the central southern counties. With its roots firmly set in the tradition of professional

Above left: Arthur Watson selling pigs in Newbury Cattle Market in the 1920s. **Top:** *Frank Neate selling Williams' Roundabouts in the 1920s.* **Below:** *Cheap Street showing the firm's offices in the 1920s.*

The company that never leaves its customers out in the cold

Ask most people in Britain what BMC General Motors used to make - or General Motors, for that matter - and they will say 'cars'. But staff at NRS' headquarters in Newbury might well give a different answer:- refrigeration equipment and cars. This is correct, and the reason for the dual interest is that piston compressors have a great deal in common with piston car engines, so development of the one is a natural extension of the development of the other. So Frigidaire came into being as the refrigeration division of General Motors, while Prestcold (PREssed STeel COmpany) began life in 1934 when a special production line was set up at Cowley to make refrigerators.

From here Prestcold went on to establish itself as a manufacturer in its own right. Then, in order to be able to provide a full range of refrigeration service, the company set up Prestcold Refrigeration Contracting (PRC) which operated from 50 depots, selling Prestcold products and also providing contracting and servicing facilities. Unfortunately contractors were wary of buying components and equipment from PRC, as not only did they have little

Above: *An early Prestcold advertisement.*
Right: *A Prestcold refrigerator in the 1950s.*
Below: *The Prestcold factory in Theale.*

choice, but the fact that it only sold its own brand was perceived as a conflict of interest. So in the late 70s Prestcold provided an alternative in the form of Nationwide Refrigeration Supplies (NRS), which was still a division of Prestcold but sold a variety of commercial refrigeration equipment and components from a range of manufacturers.

A few years later, in 1981, the Prestcold group of companies was purchased by Suter Plc from British Leyland, as BMC was known at that time; Prestcold Manufacturing and Contracting was subsequently re-sold two years later, which presented NRS with the opportunity to establish itself as a truly independent refrigeration wholesaler.

Over the next decade and a half, the 12 branches which formed the entire NRS network in 1983 grew into 31, representing the widest geographical spread of outlets of any distributor in the industry, with nationwide coverage extending from Aberdeen to Exeter. In the early years of its

sectors, catering, leisure, brewing and medical. Depending on location, customers may opt for door-to-door delivery, or they may prefer to use the traditional trade counter or a self-service outlet; whatever their requirements for delivery and availability, NRS can oblige. The entire company is geared up to meet customer requirements, and it is this which has driven its business strategy to invest in the wider network of outlets than any other distributor in the industry; in a large fleet of delivery vehicles; in specialist technical support, a 24-hour emergency service and an on-going customer care programme, sustained by a policy of continuous investment in logistics and technology. And regular customer research is carried out, just to make absolutely certain that its service continues to match customer expectations and requirements.

At the hub of the entire operation is NRS' Head Office site on Bone Lane, Newbury. Here the company has 50,000 square feet of warehousing and a custom-built production unit, in addition to its administration and distribution centre; in all, some 75 people are employed on the site, representing 30 per cent of NRS' total workforce.

Today NRS is firmly established as the industry's leading wholesaler and distributor in the UK. The company has reached this position by continuing to deliver high quality products and services; it has never compromised on quality, and it has developed a business strategy which ensures that customer requirements are always met. To further ensure this, the company has set up a website at www.nrs-wholesale.co.uk. NRS's success is well-deserved and will continue far into the future. And NRS still sells Prestcold refrigeration equipment and spares for models supplied in the 1950s!

growth, NRS pioneered the concept of satellite branches, believing that there was considerable advantage in setting up small sites close to their customers; it also introduced self-service style outlets, and went on to instigate the first 24 hour Emergency Service.

During this period the product range extended out from its primary focus on equipment to cover a full and comprehensive list of components, accessories, refrigerant and other items, in conformity with the company's policy of keeping up long-standing supplier relationships and supplying only market-leading brands.

More recently, the Company has diversified into the Air Conditioning market. A separate, dedicated division was set up in 1996 to cater for this rapidly-expanding market; subsequently the Air Conditioning division was merged into the rest of the business in order to give NRS customers the convenience of one-stop shopping. So now, whether they need to call upon NRS's traditional specialism in commercial refrigeration products and services, whether their need is for air conditioning, or whether they require a combination of the two, all their requirements can be sourced through the one supplier. NRS distributes packaged refrigeration and air conditioning equipment suitable for a wide variety of applications. Markets include the retail

Top: *Early promotion.*
Above left: *The trade counter.*
Below: *Today's fleet.*

Floruit Floreat - as it has flourished so shall it flourish

The White Hart building has been one of Newbury's best-known landmarks for many a century. Dating back to the early 1500s and originally known as the White Hart Inn, it was historically the town's coaching inn where coaching companies made an overnight stop on the way to Bath, and where travellers bound for London used to gather to take the 'Flying Coach'. These innovative four-wheeled Stage Chaises were capable of conveying four passengers to London in 12 hours, at a fare of 10 shillings (50p) each, and continued in service until Palmer's new mail coaches took over in 1784. Then in the early 19th century the White Hart Inn became the meeting-place for another group of people; the 'Loyal Berks Lodge of Hope' was formed in 1816, and the freemasons used the White Hart as their first Newbury venue, in keeping with the masons' early tradition of meeting on licensed premises. The Inn was later renamed the White Hart Hotel, and much later still, in 1924, renovations were carried out during the course of which an original window frame was removed which dated back to the year 1516.

> *Gardner Leader could equally well have pursued a career on the stage*

Meanwhile, a short distance away on the Water Bridge, above Liddiards the butcher's, a solicitors' practice had been established by George Gardner Leader in 1895. George Gardner Leader was a colourful character: a London solicitor, he could equally well have pursued a career on the stage as he had an excellent baritone voice and frequently appeared in concerts. He was very well-connected in society and was instrumental in setting up the Newbury Racecourse Company under the patronage of Edward VII; and by the time the racecourse held its first meeting in 1905 he had married the daughter of John Porter, one of the best-known racehorse trainers of the era. The origins of the Practice were therefore closely linked with the racing industry, and this connection was preserved for many years through Archie and Roland Hills; Archie was the secretary of the Racecourse for 30 years and his son Roland worked in the Practice for 40 years. In his day he was the leading

Below: *The firm's first premises on the Water Bridge, above Liddiards the butchers.*

advocate, and was once famously described by the Lord Chief Justice as a 'silver-tongued advocate' when he had managed to persuade the local magistrates to find a client not guilty, very much against the weight of evidence!

By the time of the founder's death in 1926, his firm was well-established in Newbury, dealing with property, litigation and company work, and it continued to grow until in 1951 larger premises were required. The White Hart public house offered an ideal location; the building itself was eminently suitable for conversion into offices, and its location was perfect, being in the Market Place right in the heart of Newbury. In addition to refurbishing the interior Gardner Leader undertook a complete external redecoration; and so this fine building began a new era in its history. The tavern sign depicting a white hart which can be seen in the centre window of the top floor represents an attractive link with the past, and is in fact one of the oldest tavern signs in Newbury.

Today the customers who pass through the door of the White Hart may or may not be freemasons, and they are likely to be looking not for transport, lodging or refreshment, but for expert legal advice and representation on a wide range of matters. With eight partners and over 50 staff, and additional offices in Thatcham and Hungerford, Gardner Leader offers expertise in all areas, including accident and personal injury claims, civil and criminal litigation, company and commercial law, employment matters, commercial and domestic conveyancing, family law, leases and tenancy agreements, and Wills, Trusts and Probates. Every client is assured of an efficient and quality service with a personal touch; the Practice has always been run very much as a 'family firm'. The present partners believe that people will continue to value the quality of service and individual attention which a local firm provides. To assist with this the branches at Thatcham and Hungerford are connected to the Newbury central office by high-speed computer links, providing a gateway for easy access to the specialist skills of partners and other qualified staff wherever they may be located. As this book goes to press the Practice has just established its Internet website at www.gardner-leader.co.uk which provides information of interest to both local and international clients. From its founding the proprietors of Gardner Leader have been dedicated to the tradition of service to the local community. This is demonstrated not only by their involvement in local affairs over the years but also by the esteem of other professionals and the townspeople of Newbury. It is in maintaining this and building on the virtues of their predecessors with a forward thinking team that the partners expect the firm to serve the people of Newbury, Thatcham and Hungerford for at least the next century and beyond.

Top: *Mr George Gardner Leader is fourth from the left in this 1920s picture.*
Above left: *White Hart House in 1906.*

Those with long enough memories might recall the gales and torrential rain which wreaked havoc in September 1935, and the 12 inches snow which covered Newbury three winters later. The next decade brought more havoc: in 1947 sheep, cattle and crops were lost in the floods, and a meals-on-wheels operation organised by Jack Hole brought help to those worst affected. Then there was the Berkshire tornado in May 1950, and more heavy snow in 1952 …

Acknowledgments

The publishers would like to thank the following for their help

in the production of this book

Jack Hole

Jim Irving

Paul Cannon

West Berkshire Heritage Service

Thanks are also due to Margaret Wakefield who penned the text